DATE DUE			

Stumpwork

MURIEL BEST

Stumpwork
Historical & Contemporary
Raised Embroidery

B.T. Batsford Ltd · London

ISBN 0 7134 5572 1

Typeset by Servis Filmsetting Ltd, Manchester
and printed in Great Britain by
R.J. Acford
Chichester Sussex
for the publishers
B.T. Batsford Ltd
4 Fitzhardinge Street
London W1H 0AH

CONTENTS

ACKNOWLEDGEMENTS

In writing this book I have been encouraged by the interest and help of many people who have given generously of their time. It is impossible to mention everyone individually, but I would like to thank the Curator of the Embroiderers' Guild, Louise Hamer; the Textile Curator of the Dorset County Museum, Jennifer Best; and my friends Margaret Rivers and Margaret Blow for all their help with research. I am also grateful to my friends Marjorie Barnard and Vicky Lugg, who acted as my 'readers', and I appreciate the interest and help of Mary-Dick Digges and Wilkie Smith.

My thanks, too, to Philip and Antony Best for some of the colour photography, to Jim Pascoe for his patient and cheerful help with the black-and-white photography, and to all those embroiderers who have kindly lent me work to be photographed.

Lastly, my appreciation to my husband Philip and my sons David and Antony for their advice and support; and to my editor Rachel Wright for her patience and understanding.

FOREWORD

The aim of this book is to explain the background to the highly decorative technique of seventeenth century raised embroidery, which has become known as stumpwork; and to show the present-day embroiderer ways of using some of the methods in contemporary work.

The book is divided into two sections, the first dealing with seventeenth-century stumpwork and the second with its modern counterpart. An historical background is provided for the period when this form of embroidery was at its most popular, with an outline of its origins, materials and stitches. Individual caskets, mirror frames and pictures are described, and a guide is given to the whereabouts of surviving examples.

In the second section of the book, the use of modern materials, methods and stitches in contemporary stumpwork are explained, with advice on planning an embroidery. The work of modern embroiderers, who have put their own interpretation on the theme of stumpwork, is described in detail, and a reading list completes the book.

Stumpwork is enjoying a revival, and it is hoped that the reader will be inspired to try this fascinating technique of embroidery.

INTRODUCTION

The definition of stumpwork given in Chambers' *Twentieth Century Dictionary* is 'elaborate raised embroidery of the fifteenth to seventeenth centuries using various materials, and raised by stumps of wood or pads of wool'. Obviously there is rather more to it than one might imagine from that description. The actual term 'stumpwork' was first used in the nineteenth century to describe the intricate embroidery of the mid-seventeenth century, possibly because small stumps of wood were used to raise parts of the embroidery, in particular the hands and faces of the figures. Caulfield and Saward mention raised work/stumpwork in their *Dictionary of Needlework*, published in 1882. Lady Marian Alford also refers to raised work, calling it 'embroidery on the stamp' in her book *Needlework as Art*, written in 1886.

The period of stumpwork's greatest popularity was from 1650 to 1680, and the embroidered pieces were used for either pictures, caskets or mirror frames. For the most part this highly decorative form of needlework appears to have been the work of young girls who, having been instructed in the basic techniques and stitches of embroidery, would then put their expertise to more creative ends using their samplers as a reference. It is not difficult to imagine how eagerly, released from the restrictions of their samplers, they assembled the fabrics, silks, spangles, purls and beads for their new projects. For them it must have been the equivalent of playing with dolls' houses; fashioning little figures, dressing them in lavish costume, and placing them in an elaborate setting amid tiny castles, trees, and flowers with a wealth of animals, birds and insects. The discrepancies in scale, the assorted collection of kings and queens, the insects as big as animals, and the fantastic birds inhabiting an enchanted landscape, evoke a world reminiscent of Lewis Carroll's *Alice in Wonderland*. It is interesting to speculate whether he had in fact seen any examples of stumpwork.

Wealthy households in the seventeenth century usually employed a resident tutor whose job it was to supervise all the needlework, both practical and decorative. The tutor would instruct the servants in the making and repairing of household linen, and also teach fine embroidery to the daughters of the house. One such teacher, Hannah Senior, entered the service of the Earl of Thomond to teach his daughters the use of the needle at the salary of £200 per annum. This was a generous sum at that time, compared to the stipend of a clergyman, who earned between £40 and £100 according to the size and location of his parish. Unfortunately for Hannah, however, the Earl did not honour this agreement. The outraged Hannah petitioned for leave to sue him, but this was refused. A Mrs Hutchison in her *Memoirs* lists among eight tutors that she had at the age of seven, one employed solely to teach needlework.

Stumpwork, called raised or 'embosted' work in the seventeenth century, was prized even in those

1 Sampler, mid-seventeenth century, worked on linen in coloured silks and silver gilt thread, with some raised and padded work. (*Burrell Collection, Glasgow Art Gallery and Museum*)

Our concern for the conservation of our needlework heritage has led to preservation of the condition of old embroideries by controlling their exposure to light and atmosphere. By studying these old embroideries we can discover the ingenious methods used to create a sculpted look in low relief, and the stitches which were used to embellish the padded areas. Some examples which are not so well preserved nevertheless provide interesting information on the working methods, and are well worth careful study. Fascinating glimpses of the design drawn out on the background fabric show how the embroiderer has often added improvisations and slightly altered the original concept. It is quite common to see padding exposed where the stitching has worn away; sometimes the former will be animal wool enclosed in linen, and sometimes bundles of linen thread couched in position with a similar thread. A casket in the Holborne of Menstrie Museum in Bath shows how this method of raising the surface has been used for the small castles. They are all highly raised, and where the detached buttonhole stitch has worn away in places the linen thread padding is revealed underneath. A fragment in the collection of the Embroiderers' Guild has a cartouche raised from the surface by the same technique and over this is an elaborate decoration of stiffened loops couched round the frame. The loops themselves are made from very narrow strips of vellum or parchment, closely wrapped with a fine thread. This particular technique seems to have been very popular and occurs frequently on pictures and caskets. Embroiderers today often wrap thin strips of card with thread to make frames for their work, and history once again proves that nothing is new. Even painting on fabric was used in the seventeenth century, and skies were often left painted blue instead of embroidered.

The decline of stumpwork towards the end of the seventeenth century was no doubt due to the mounting interest in all things Chinese. The vogue for *chinoiserie* influenced both furniture and furnishings, and embroiderers were soon following the current style. The excellent craftsmanship, the wonderful colours and exotic designs were so

days, and the many fine examples still in existence owe their quality to the fact that special covers or cases were often made to protect them. Many pictures, caskets and mirror frames are now on display in museums, art galleries and in stately homes, where they can be seen and appreciated by the public. Private owners will occasionally put items from their collections on display, or let them be viewed by special appointment.

2 Casket, English, 1650–1700, worked in silks. The
embroidery tells the story of Eliezer and Rebekah.
(*Burrell Collection, Glasgow Art Gallery and Museum*)

different to any that had been seen before. Canvas
work once again became popular, and embroidery
was used for more practical and less decorative
purposes, for instance curtains, wall-hangings and
upholstery. Earlier this century one writer described stumpwork as being '. . . of grotesque

ugliness . . . a mockery of sculpture which departs
from the legitimate province of the needle'. Oh
dear – what a harsh, unkind statement. Fortunately everyone has different points of view, and surely
the interest shown in stumpwork today must prove
that writer's judgement to be in question.

The characteristic sculpted look of stumpwork
is being incorporated in present-day embroidery
using modern materials and threads, but it is
important to aim at a contemporary style, with

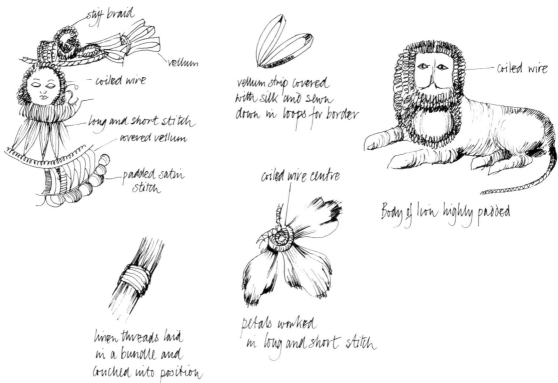

stiff braid

vellum

coiled wire

long and short stitch

covered vellum

padded satin stitch

vellum strip covered with silk and sewn down in loops for border

coiled wire centre

coiled wire

Body of lion highly padded

linen threads laid in a bundle and couched into position

petals worked in long and short stitch

3 (*Top*) Detail of a portrait panel, showing the silk-covered vellum which is folded and couched in place over a padded base of linen threads to form an elaborate cartouche. (*Embroiderers' Guild Collection*)

4 Study sheet, with drawings of details from the portrait panel in the Embroiderers' Guild Collection.

attention paid to good design and simplicity of working. There is no value in copying what has been done in the past; instead one should contrive to learn from the mistakes, and emulate the strong points. The embroideries reflected the age they lived in; time lends enchantment to their work.

Although many of the materials used in the seventeenth century are comparable with those available today, there are some modern man-made products which do the job as well, if not better. Stitches remain basically the same in principle, even if the names alter over the years.

There is always something new to discover when studying historical embroidery, and it is hoped readers will be stimulated to start their own research into this intriguing form of decorative embroidery.

Historical Background 1

To understand any of the arts it is important, and indeed interesting, to study the background against which they were produced. To place a style of embroidery in its social and historical setting is a fascinating exercise; to ask why certain techniques, materials and stitches were used, and what influenced the choice of subject.

The seventeenth century was a period of great change and upheaval in Britain. During this time there was civil war; the reigning King, Charles I, was tried by his subjects, found guilty and beheaded in 1649. His Queen, Henrietta Maria, lived in exile in France, and his eldest son Charles constantly planned to overthrow the current authority, and so to regain the throne and his right to rule his country. From 1653 to 1658 England was ruled by the Lord Protector, Oliver Cromwell; it was a time of great austerity, with furniture, furnishings and dress kept simple and functional. However, embroidery was still used for decorating household linen and domestic furnishings, and there is evidence that more elaborate embroidery was being done in some households. For instance, a stumpwork casket now in the Whitworth Art Gallery, Manchester, was worked between 1654 and 1656. Oliver Cromwell's wife is said to have employed several clergymen's daughters to do needlework.

In 1660, Monck, a professional soldier, invited Charles II to become King. General Monck, although he had served Cromwell, was convinced that if England were not to fall once more into chaos the 'old order' of the King in Parliament must be restored. With the reinstatement of the monarchy, life became more relaxed. There was a breakdown of Puritan values and rebirth of liberal thought, and in consequence taste became more extravagant, as is evident from the furnishings and costume of the day.

The century saw a marked growth in international wealth, and increased trading with other countries. In 1601 the East India Company had been formed and now spread the influence of oriental design in England. The merchant class had become more powerful and wealthy, so it was no longer only the nobility who had money and leisure to indulge in all aspects of the arts. Drama, music and literature all flourished. The Restoration comedies that were so popular then are still attracting audiences today.

The court also had close links with its French counterpart, and this influence, too, can be seen in the decorative arts. The painters Claude and Poussin were at the height of their careers, and Peter Lely was kept busy painting the many court beauties of the day. Many of these paintings can be seen at Hampton Court Palace; the elaborate costume, ringletted hairstyles, and plump pouting faces seem far removed from our ideas of beauty now.

The architect Sir Christopher Wren was an influential figure, planning the rebuilding of much

5 Women's hairstyles in the seventeenth century. The hair was worn in ringlets which framed the face, and the hair at the back was usually coiled into a bun worn high on the head. Costume for both men and women was often elaborately decorated with lace, even to the tops of the men's boots. The costume of a noblewoman had a soft skirt looped back to reveal the petticoat. A square handkerchief folded diagonally was sometimes worn above a square-necked bodice with a long stiffened stomacher. The two-tiered sleeves were edged with lace.

16

of the city after the Great Fire of London in 1666. Stone replaced wooden structures, and this material, together with the classical lines of Wren's buildings, completely changed the face of London, which rapidly replaced Amsterdam as the major trading city of Europe.

During this time Robert Boyle and Isaac Newton were making important scientific discoveries. The Royal Society was founded in 1660 and the King became its Fundator or founder; in 1662 he granted the royal charter, and he continued a most interested and encouraging patron.

An important record of everyday life in England is contained within the pages of Samuel Pepys' diaries. As First Lord of the Admiralty he mixed in privileged circles; grand state occasions are recorded, intermingled with the intriguing trivia of domestic life in the seventeenth century; not to mention titbits of gossip about prominent figures in society. He particularly admired the 'lovely Lady Castlemaine', his favourite among the royal mistresses, and even went so far as to buy a portrait of her, one of the numerous copies made by Peter Lely for her admirers.

From the mid century to 1700 tremendous changes took place which are responsible for much of the structure of our society today. The modern arrangement of our meals – breakfast, lunch and dinner – dates from this time; pottery and glass replaced pewter and wood at table. At Chatsworth the Duke of Devonshire even installed a bath with hot and cold running water. Merchants were as rich as peers, and some evidently made money from judicious marriages; to quote Mr Emmanuel Badd of the Isle of Wight, 'By God's blessing and loss of five wives, I grew very rich.'

Towards the end of Charles II's reign tension grew between the rising Protestant faction and the ruling classes with their leanings towards Catholicism and the High Church, and subsequently

6 Portrait of Lady Castlemaine (Barbara Cleveland), after Peter Lely. Lady Castlemaine was a court beauty who became the mistress of Charles II. (*National Portrait Gallery, London*)

relations between King and Parliament deteriorated. After his death in 1685 Charles was succeeded by his Roman Catholic brother, James II, who ruled until his deposition in the Glorious Revolution of 1688, which brought the Protestant William and Mary to the throne. Thus England became a constitutional monarchy and a remarkable period in British history ended. There was no doubt that with the restoration of Charles II, there had been an awakening from a dull and prosaic way of living, and that his enthusiasm influenced many aspects of the country's life.

2
Origins of stumpwork

Before stumpwork became popular for domestic embroidery in Britain it was being used extensively on the Continent for ecclesiastical work, and was termed *brodées en relief*. Often church vestments combined laid gold thread with highly padded figures. These were modelled on the background material with the aid of additional fabric, cardboard, leather, and hemp, over which would be placed silk, satin and couched metal thread.

The fabric was often painted or embroidered to emphasize the fall of pleats on garments and the lines and wrinkles on faces. The hair and beards would be made of metal thread wrapped with braid (*fils de fer enroulés de ganses brunes*); the highly padded shapes were usually outlined with metal thread. The work was done by professionals working in embroidery studios. They looked towards sculpture for their inspiration, and consequently the figures were modelled very realistically using card, leather and hemp, stuck with paste and then covered in couched metal thread. Much of this elaborate work was done in the fifteenth century, a period noted for its great riches and fine houses, all of which were reflected in the embroideries, where lavish use was made of beautiful lace, silk brocade, precious stones and gold leaf.

A particularly fine example of this rich and intricate work is seen on a Czech chasuble originally made for Brno Cathedral in 1487. The ground fabric is violet-coloured satin on which are applied the figures of the Virgin Mary and St Venceslas surrounded by angels. All the ornamentation, the rich gowns of the figures and the bands of inscriptions in the angels' hands, give the impression of the Gothic style. The chasuble is now in the Museum of Decorative Arts in Brno.

Another interesting example of relief or raised work is a small picture, possibly Spanish, which is in the textile collection of the Lady Lever Art Gallery at Port Sunlight, Merseyside. It is dated 1650 and depicts the Holy Family with the Virgin Mary enthroned beneath God the Father and the Holy Ghost, surrounded by angels. The figures are very sculptural in style, and couched metal thread is used extensively on the background. This immensely detailed panel measures only 24 by 25.5 cm (9$\frac{1}{2}$ by 10 in.), and although the colours are considerably faded, the overall effect is very rich and lively.

Raised work in Britain is mostly domestic in origin, although some early examples originated at Little Gidding near Huntingdon, where there was a Christian community producing fine bookbindings. In 1625 Nicholas Ferrar, a brilliantly talented young man who was a Fellow of Clare College, Cambridge, and a Member of Parliament, renounced his career and worldly ambitions to found the community at Little Gidding, an estate belonging to his mother. He was joined by his brother, brother-in-law and their families, about thirty people in all. They lived in a manor house

8 The church at Little Gidding where Nicholas Ferrar and his family worshipped. The community took over a derelict medieval church and restored it. The nave and west façade were built in 1714 by Nicholas Ferrar's nephew, and the church was again restored in 1853. Although the community survived ransacking in 1646, their pattern of life changed with the death of John, Nicholas's brother. In 1969 the Little Gidding Fellowship was formed, and today in a large farmhouse built on the site of the original manor house there is another community dedicated to God and a simple way of life.

7 St Venceslas. A detail of the figure of the Saint from a chasuble dated 1487. The figure is highly padded and worked on a background of violet-coloured silk satin. (*Museum of Decorative Arts, Brno*)

not far from a chapel, and although the former has been demolished, the chapel, much restored, still remains. The family devoted itself to charitable works, to preparing harmonies of the Scriptures, to exquisite needlework, and to fine bookbinding.

Charles I visited the community several times, and a bound copy of the Harmonies of the Gospel presented to him is now housed in the British Museum in London. The married sister, Mary Collett, trained and directed the women in the making of adornments for their chapel: the tapestry curtains, altar hangings and silken carpet. All of them were exquisite needlewomen. After the death of Nicholas in 1637 the life of the community continued for a further twenty years, during which time much fine work was produced in decorative bookbinding. The threat of civil war in 1642 led the family to seek sanctuary abroad. It is probable that

9 Embroidered picture, Spanish, *c.* 1650, depicting the
Holy Family. The picture is worked on linen, with
heavily padded and raised areas and extensive use of
couched metal thread. (*Lady Lever Art Gallery, Port
Sunlight, Merseyside County Art Galleries*)

they were influenced by the *brodées en relief* that
were being worked on the Continent, and that
when they eventually returned to England and
Little Gidding in 1646 they introduced the style to
their work there. The King, now a fugitive in his
own country, sought sanctuary with them, and
three months later they paid dearly for their loyalty
when their home was raided by Puritan soldiers.
The chapel was desecrated, the house with its
many fine books and beautiful furnishings was
burnt, and the community was dispersed.

Other early examples of raised work can be
found on ecclesiastical garments and furnishings;
in Durham Cathedral there is an embroidered cope
dating from the 1630s on which some of the areas
are padded. The red silk ground is decorated with
powdered motifs including cherubs, sunbursts and
flowers, wheatears and cherubim. On the hood the
figure of David is shown holding the severed head
of Goliath. Another cope, dating from the mid-
fifteenth century, has a hood which was extensively altered in the 1630s, and this, too, has been
highly padded.

So from these early beginnings raised or
embosted work became popular for domestic
decorative embroidery, and although it was not
until the mid-seventeenth century that it reached
its peak, the embroideries of the Elizabethan
period sometimes had padded motifs, and leaves
and petals worked in detached buttonhole stitch.
The gauntlets of expensive gloves which were
given as presents usually had a design of very
decorative stitching and included some raised
work; samplers, too, often incorporated motifs in
detached buttonhole which stood away from the
background.

10 Hood of an embroidered cope dating from the 1630s,
on which some areas are raised and padded. The cope is
said to have been presented by Charles I. (*The Dean and
Chapter of Durham*)

3
Design and method
in historical work

Subject and design

Tapestries were an obvious source of inspiration for the embroideress in the seventeenth century, and many of the designs were adapted for small-scale embroideries. Stories from the Bible were particularly favoured, Susannah and the Elders, David and Bathsheba, and Esther and Ahasueras being among the most popular. However, after the Restoration the subjects ceased to be purely ecclesiastical in character, and tales from mythology were chosen, with the Virtues and the seasons of the year also being favourite subjects.

There was little regard for balanced composition and good design. Motifs were assembled in a haphazard fashion with no attention paid to relative scale; animals, fruits, flowers and insects could be as big as people. They all appear to jostle for position, and any remaining spaces were covered with spangles or peacock feathers, although the latter have long since disintegrated. The arms of the owner are occasionally introduced, and the lion, unicorn, leopard and stag frequently occur. In addition rabbits, squirrels, hares, foxes, and dogs nestle in corners. The variety of treatment and elaboration depended on the skill of the embroiderer.

In much of the work the same motifs recur. Identical castles with many turrets, and windows made from tiny pieces of mica, decorate the landscapes. The castles often stand on a grassy mound, which may be made by couching down a knotted thread or silk chenille. All manner of birds, some resembling parrots, others with crests and exotic plumage, perch in small trees or on boughs complete with oak leaves and acorns, or on grapevines hung with large bunches of grapes. A myriad of insects from ladybirds, beetles and spiders to larger caterpillars and butterflies, fill any empty spaces. Caterpillars and butterflies were symbols for Charles I and the Restoration respectively, the butterfly symbolizing the rebirth of the monarchy, and possibly showed clandestinely the family's loyalty to the Crown. It is interesting to speculate that the biblical stories might have been chosen for their political implications, as in general they depict the triumph of persecuted minorities. The sun frequently shines out from beneath the clouds, and occasionally the moon shines at the same time. These similarities suggest that the background fabric of silk or fine canvas was purchased with the design ready drawn out by a professional artist, perhaps complete with the tiny carved wooden hands and faces for the figures too. Wax moulds and wooden fruits were also used, so it is quite likely that they were all bought at the same time, rather like the present-day needlework kit. Certainly one tutor lists wax fruits amongst other needlework items on an invoice for her employer. Designs for flowers and beasts were taken from herbals, and a trade publication of the period lists 'A new book of Flowers, Beasts and

11 (*Top*) Castles and large manor houses were often set in a rural landscape. The houses reflected the architecture of the period, and plumed smoke was shown issuing from the tall chimneys.

12 Fantastic birds, some with exotic plumage, were a common feature in all stumpwork embroideries.

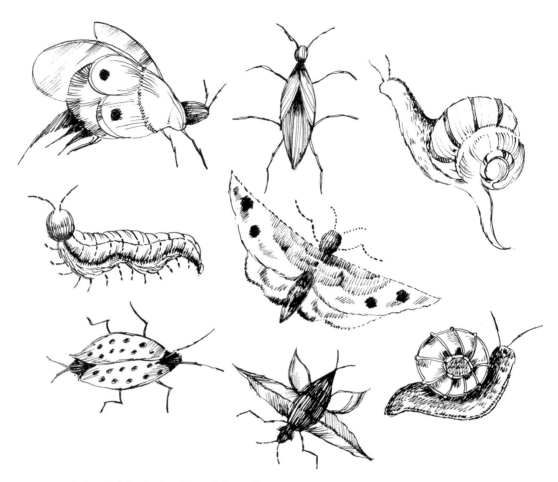

13 Insects, including ladybirds, beetles and butterflies were popular motifs, as were snails.

Birds', invented and drawn by J. Dunfall; a book of 'Branches, Slips, and Flies etc.'; 'A Book of Flora'; and a 'Book of Flowers, Beasts, Birds, and Fruits'. In all, over five hundred titles are given, including 'Kings and Queens'. There appears to have been an abundance of designs for the embroiderer's reference.

Topiary and tree grafting were innovations in the seventeenth century, and the trends are reflected in the embroideries, together with a profusion of flowers which were in favour; these included roses, honeysuckle, carnations, pansies, iris, cornflowers, bluebells and solanum. Orna-mental gardens in the Italian style were in vogue for the wealthy, and these, too, often feature in the designs. Miniature fountains adorn small pools, in which swim tiny fish. The pools themselves are surrounded by rocks forming a grotto, or sometimes the voluptuous figure of Bathsheba bathes in the pool attended by her handmaidens. Bathsheba invariably holds a mirror in her hand in which her face is reflected. The small puppet-like figures are dressed in the costume of the seventeenth century, which adds to their quaintness. The figures are often modelled on Charles I and Henrietta Maria, or on Charles II and Catherine of Braganza; sometimes there are discrepancies in the costume so that the king will be dressed in the fashion of the 1640s and the queen in the style of the 1660s, or vice

14 (*Top*) Casket top showing Bathsheba bathing in a pool, attended by her handmaiden. The two figures are worked in flat stitchery, contrasting with the raised areas of the other motifs. (*Embroiderers' Guild Collection*)

15 Detail of the casket top in fig. 14, showing the figure of David seated beneath a canopy. (*Embroiderers' Guild Collection*)

16 The top of a casket worked by Anne Mairy Sawell in 1672. The background is silk with raised and padded areas and extensive use of coiled wire, sometimes known as bullion. The figures are thought to represent Charles II and his Queen, Catherine. (*Lady Lever Art Gallery, Port Sunlight*)

versa. The main figure of the king is generally seated beneath a canopy which is raised from the surface by means of paper placed under it. This also provided some protection for the elaborate figure, preventing the delicate stitching from being rubbed. The tents seen in the embroideries reflect the fashion of the time, since whenever the Court journeyed around the country, tents and their elaborate trimmings formed an essential part of the travelling equipment. Although the same motifs repeatedly occur, there are of course some exceptions. A panel in the Lady Lever Art Gallery, Port Sunlight, tells the story of the overthrow of Pharaoh and his host in the Red Sea. Another unmounted panel in the Victoria & Albert Museum, London, is a portrait of a lady in an oval frame with a shepherd and shepherdess tending their sheep in the background; outside the oval in each corner there is a cherub's head. These are also raised from the surface, covered with silk and the features embroidered on top; they each seem to have a curious sardonic expression. In spite of their

17 A picture dating from 1669–79, worked by Damaris Pearse, with raised and padded areas. It tells the story of the drowning of Pharaoh and his host. (*Lady Lever Art Gallery, Port Sunlight*)

lack of a cohesive design, these stumpwork embroideries have great charm and story-telling qualities; there is always something new to discover that may have been missed on first viewing.

Materials, methods and stitches

The background fabric for most of the embroideries was a fine linen canvas or an ivory-coloured silk. Occasionally the silk was darned with a silk thread in a diaper pattern, which added extra richness. The design would be drawn in outline on to the background using ink or watercolour. Small crosses and circles indicated where to place motifs and spangles, and also provided a key for stitches and colour. Sometimes areas would be shaded with colour, and often the blue skies were left unworked. It is still possible to see these outlines on some of the embroideries where the stitching or applied shape has not quite matched up with the design underneath. It seems that most backgrounds were prepared by professional artists, since the drawing is that of a practised hand.

On to the prepared background a wealth of coloured silks, fine wools, metal threads, beads, spangles, and tiny seed pearls would be applied. Coiled and plaited wire and flat metal plate were constantly used for borders and elaborate cartouches. Thin strips of vellum or parchment closely bound with silk were folded and looped into a variety of patterns, held in place by couching stitches. A fine copper wire wrapped with a fine silk thread and then tightly coiled around something akin to a fine knitting needle was often

18 (*Top*) Detail from the side of a casket, showing a fantastic bird with part of the wings and the tail standing away from the background. (*On loan to the Dorset Natural History and Archaeological Society, Dorset County Museum, Dorchester*)

19 A detail from the casket in fig. 18, taken from the top and showing a padded leopard covered in detached buttonhole stitch.

20 (*Top*) Casket, mid-seventeenth century, showing the top. The king is seated beneath a canopy surrounded by his entourage. All the figures are raised from the background. (*York Castle Museum*)

21 Detail of the figure of the king. The head is padded, with the features embroidered on top. Flat stitchery is used for the background, and detached buttonhole stitch for part of the clothing and the draperies.

couched into leaf shapes and used for decorative borders.

A variety of stitches was used and included detached buttonhole, satin, chain, stem, couching, speckling, rococo, holly, plaited braid, laid work, french knots and bullion knots. Of these, detached buttonhole is the most versatile and frequently used; the highly padded beasts, birds, and fruits were usually covered with this stitch, as were leaves and the petals of flowers. In some cases a fine wire was used to outline the edges of leaves and petals, in order to make them stand away from the background. Underneath, the shape would be echoed by repeating the motif in flat surface stitchery, usually satin or long and short stitch. Knotted silks were used for foliage and grassy banks, together with darned silk pile which resembled chenille.

Figures and ornaments were made by cutting out the shapes in linen, which were then stretched over card and padded with either horsehair or animal wool. Paper was pasted on to the back to prevent the linen from fraying. The finished piece was then applied to the background with small slip stitches. The faces and hands of the figures were carved from wood or ivory, or sometimes fashioned in wax. The faces were either painted, covered with close satin stitch, or, most commonly, covered with silk and the features embroidered. The faces are amazingly expressive considering the small scale, and two sets of eyebrows were used to convey a look of surprise. The hands were usually left uncovered. The ones carved from wood were long and elegant with straight fingers, but sometimes the hands were made from covered wire with each finger separate from the other, and these would be curled round to hold objects such as shepherds' crooks, daggers, letters etc. ·

The clothing of the figures copied the fashion of the seventeenth century. Shepherds and shepherdesses were dressed in the simple garments of country folk, whilst the people of the court were lavishly arrayed in silk brocade and lace. The dresses of silk were sometimes embroidered to look like patterned brocade, and the men's costume was often worked in detached buttonhole stitch. Delicate needle-made lace decorated necklines and the edges of cuffs, and seed pearls and tiny pieces of coral all added to the sumptuous effect. The figures were nearly always assembled in the same way, but of course there were exceptions, and occasionally figures were built up by laying bundles of thread together, couched in position and then covered with fabric. These figures seldom have the same attention to detail, and appear to be the work of less skilled embroiderers.

Separately worked motifs stitched on fine linen canvas in tent stitch were cut out and then applied to the background fabric with small slip stitches. They were then outlined with a fine silk thread or cord. These were termed 'slips'. Usually they were left flat to the surface, but some were padded with animal wool. Work that has been left unfinished quite often has just the slips completed and sewn in place, with perhaps a thread hanging as though waiting for the owner to take up the needle again.

4

Caskets, mirror frames and pictures

Stumpwork was not used merely for ornamental pictures, but the finished embroidery was also employed for more practical purposes, including cushions, purses, gloves, mirror frames and caskets.

Caskets

These were used to hold a variety of objects; some were designed as writing cabinets to contain paper, ink wells, seals and sand boxes (filled with sand for blotting letters); others held jewellery, silver pins, brooches and scent bottles, and of course some were solely for needlework tools and threads. The embroidery was worked on linen or silk in separate panels for the sides, top and the edgings of the lid, and the inside panels decorating the drawers were often worked in a flat long stitch with a floss silk thread. The designs on these inside panels would usually be a formal geometric pattern or stylized flowers and leaves.

When the embroidered panels were complete they were sent away to a cabinet maker, who mounted and fitted them to the chosen shape. The actual style of the cabinet varied, the earlier ones

22 A small purse, mid-seventeenth century, based on a design of grapes, which have been padded and covered with detached buttonhole stitch. (*Victoria & Albert Museum, London*)

being less elaborate. Some were simply a rectangular box with a plain lid, like a miniature chest. Later the caskets became more complex, with flaps that let down, or doors which opened to reveal a tiny set of drawers. Inevitably the caskets would contain a 'secret' compartment to hide away special treasures. The lids of more complicated caskets had sloping sides, rising steeply as in the roof of a house. Inside some, there were also little trays divided into small compartments to hold tiny objects. These trays would lift out to reveal a space for storing larger items. Silver, or silver-plated, locks and handles were attached, and most caskets had four ball-feet, made either of silver or wood. The lining of the drawers and trays was usually of silk, either red, pink or blue, the last not in use until after 1650. Patterned or marbled paper was used at the base, and sometimes on the inside of the lid, where a small mirror might be mounted.

The outside edges of the box were bordered with braid or gimp, and these varied from a simple neat band to a more complicated lacy trimming of gold thread. The very ornate braids appear coarse and gaudy in contrast to the delicate stitching of the embroidery. The same style of figures and motifs are used to decorate the caskets as were used in the pictures, and often a complete story would unfold as different scenes were depicted on each side and the top. The figures on the lids of the boxes were frequently framed in an elaborate cartouche.

Occasionally the embroiderer would include the date and her initials in the work. Many of these charming caskets are the work of unknown embroiderers, but where they have been handed down through families as precious heirlooms it may be possible to know something about the industrious needleworker. Two famous examples are Martha Edlin and Hannah Smith, whose work can be seen in the Victoria & Albert Museum in London, and the Whitworth Art Gallery, Manchester, respectively. Martha Edlin was a most prolific and talented embroiderer. By the age of

23 Needlework bird, c. 1700, designed as a small gift or thimble case. It is worked in detached buttonhole stitch using silk and metal threads over a padded mould. The bird is entirely free-standing and measures 12.7 cm (5 in.) long. (*Burrell Collection, Glasgow Art Gallery and Museum*)

24 Casket, mid-seventeenth century. The two front doors open to reveal three drawers and a wide shallow tray, lined with pale blue silk. The interior of the lid is padded and quilted, with space left for a mirror. The embroidery tells the story of the Shunamite woman. (*York Castle Museum*)

eight she had finished her sampler of a dozen or more beautifully worked bands of ornament and three alphabets in coloured silk threads on a linen background. The work is signed and dated 1668. In the following year she completed a whitework sampler of open-work lace patterns and bands of embroidery in white threads. With all this exemplary work finished she began the panels for her casket, which apparently took her two years to complete, as it is dated 1671. The cabinet has a shaped top, the sides of which slope inwards to support the lid. Around the sides of the box are panels showing scenes from the Old Testament; these are embroidered on linen with tent stitch in

silk threads, and further decorated with metal purl, silk cord and detached buttonhole stitch. Above these panels there is a band of laid and couched work, and the sloping sides at the top are embroidered with motifs of animals including a lion, a unicorn and a camel. These are worked in a variety of stitches, with a further narrow band of laid work forming the sides of the lid. The top is worked in the same manner as the sides and base of the casket.

Obviously idle hands had to be kept busy, and work began on another flat, oblong box, this time in silk embroidery and beadwork on white satin. Surely after this her training was complete. Martha Edlin can have had no idea that over three hundred years later people would be treasuring and marvelling at her exquisite work.

The casket made by Hannah Smith is similar in style to the one by Martha, although it was worked ten years earlier. The box is of the same construction, with sloping sides at the top narrowing inwards to a smaller lid. The panels are embroidered with episodes from the Bible and scenes of autumn and winter. The casket is worked in silk, gilt and silver on linen and satin. A letter was found in one of the drawers written in a neat hand by Hannah, in which she describes how she went to Oxford when she was almost twelve years of age, and how she remained there for two years from 1654 to 1656, and during that time completed her 'cabinette'.

A casket in the Holborne of Menstrie Museum in Bath is dated 1660 and has country themes embroidered on the side panels. There are shep-

25 Casket, 1650–1700, showing the sloping top which was popular. It is worked in silks and metal thread on a background of silk satin, and tells the story of Eliezer's search for a wife for Isaac. (*Burrell Collection, Glasgow Art Gallery and Museum*)

26 Casket, 1671, worked by Martha Edlin. The top has sloping sides, and the casket is decorated with scenes from the Old Testament. (*Victoria & Albert Museum, London*)

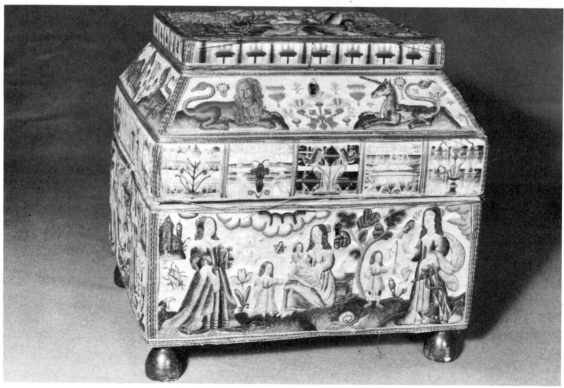

27 (*Top*) Casket, mid-seventeenth century. The figures of Charles I and his Queen are padded and stand within a raised border of metal plate couched down in a basketweave pattern. (*On loan to the Dorset Natural History and Archaeological Society, Dorset County Museum, Dorchester*)

28 Detail from the front of the casket in fig. 27, showing a manor house with open doors worked in detached buttonhole stitch. To the right of the house is the keyhole for locking the cabinet.

29 On the back of the casket from fig. 27 is a floral design worked in flat stitchery.

herds piping to their flocks, milkmaids milking cows, and four men in a small boat rowing on the river. The front of the casket shows the ladies of the court in their dresses. The panel on the lid shows a hunting scene contained within an elaborate frame. This differs from the rest of the embroidery in that it is worked in tent stitch. The edges of the casket are banded with tortoiseshell.

There are many fine caskets in both public and private collections, and whether they are in good condition or not, they are all well worth study. An exceptional example is housed in the reserve collection of Dorset County Museum, and is on loan from the family of Major-General Mark Bond. The quality of the workmanship is superb and the colours remain as true and as fresh now as they must have been when they were sewn. The casket is a simple rectangular shape, but the interior is at present a mystery, for although the lock has a key, it refuses to open! The shape of the box suggests that it might contain a tray divided into compartments which lifts out to reveal storage space underneath. There is a glimpse of marbled paper on the outside of the box at the bottom edge, and this might very well be used to line part of the interior. The sides of the casket are decorated with highly raised figures in splendid costume, except for the back which has a design of stylized flowers. In its centre is a basket fashioned of strips of metal plate bound closely with silk thread. The plate is crimped and couched in position with a matching thread. The basket is filled with flowers and leaves, and flanked on either side by a large flower. The front panel has two figures set against a landscape with a grand house in the centre standing on a hill; the doors, worked in detached buttonhole stitch, stand away from the background as though they were ajar, and smoke pours from the chimneys. Oak trees with outsize leaves are set in the landscape, and a fantastic bird, with large wings, a

30 A detail from the side of the casket, showing the use of detached buttonhole stitch for the tree, butterfly and flower contrasting with the flat stitchery on the figure.

curly tail and a crest, stands between the figures. One of the figures wears a crown edged with seed pearls, and a tiny necklace of pearls. Her dress is very full, hanging in folds, and resembles a patterned brocade; the overskirt is worked in detached buttonhole stitch in shades of pink. In her hand she holds a sceptre. The other figure has a plainer dress, but it is also decorated with seed pearls. In her long elegant hands she holds a scroll and a spear.

Two different scenes decorate the remaining sides. On one there is the gruesome sight of Judith holding a sword in one hand and the severed head of Holofernes in the other. She is standing in a pleasant landscape surrounded by leaves, flowers and insects, and in one corner there is a pool complete with fishes. On her other side stand a large bird and a unicorn, roughly similar in size!

On the opposite side of the casket is another rural scene, with the figure of Jael in the centre holding a tent peg in one hand and a hammer in the other with the intention of smiting a blow into the head of the sleeping general Sisera, although Jael looks almost benign in this embroidery. On the right a deer lies down beside her, while a fantastic bird is perched on a branch to her left. On the lid of the casket are the figures of Charles I and his Queen standing in front of two castles with the sun peeping out from the clouds. An oval frame surrounds them, and this, again, is metal plate, which is wrapped with silk and couched down to resemble basket-work. The frame is enfolded with leaves, flowers and pomegranates. In the top corners there are two exotic-looking birds with outstretched wings, and in the corresponding lower corners are a leopard and a lion. Any remaining spaces are filled with snails, butterflies and beetles. The edges of the lid are decorated with flowers and leaves in a scroll design worked in flat long and short stitch. The whole casket is trimmed along the edges with a neat silver-gilt braid. Altogether this is a most delightful and superb example of raised work at its very best.

Mirror frames

Mirror frames vary considerably in their construction, but basically they consist of a board about one and a half inches deep into which the glass is sunk to a depth of about half an inch. The framework is covered with silk or velvet and bound with gold or silver braid. In some cases an extra frame of real or imitation tortoiseshell surrounds the embroidered panels. The quicksilvering of glass dates from the sixteenth century, and as mirror glass was still expensive the actual mirrors were often quite small with a wide border of elaborate needlework to make them appear larger and more imposing. With stumpwork embroideries, it is curious that it is the borders for mirror frames which are the most likely to be unfinished. One such frame in the Victoria & Albert Museum even has a thread of silk left in mid-stitch. Some of the slips have been worked and stitched in position, with some surface stitchery added. The design is quite clearly drawn out on to the background of white silk, and looks like the work of a professional artist. Why was it abandoned? Whatever happened to the embroiderer? Perhaps enthusiasm for the project just ran out; it remains a mystery. The design of this frame contains many familiar motifs; there is a grand house at the centre top with smoke pouring from the chimneys. To one side of the house stands a tree under which lurks an enormous caterpillar; beyond this is a slip in the form of a rose, with a similar one on the opposite side. At the bottom there is an ornamental pond, complete with fountain and two fish. The pond is surrounded by rocks, and at the other side are decorative flowers in the form of applied slips. The figures are drawn out, but no attempt has been made to do any stitching on them. This particular mirror frame is a typical example of the way in which the various motifs would be arranged. Castles or great houses

31 Details from an unfinished mirror frame in the Victoria & Albert Museum, showing a large house at the top above which the sun shines through the clouds, and at the bottom a decorative fountain surrounded by rocks and coral.

32 Mirror frame, mid-seventeenth century, decorated with scenes of the Nativity in padded and raised embroidery on a silk background. (*Victoria & Albert Museum, London*)

33 Detail from the mirror frame in fig. 32, showing a bird sitting on a grapevine. The bird is worked in detached buttonhole stitch with the wings standing away from the background. The branch is of couched metal thread, and the leaves and grapes are worked in detached buttonhole stitch. The base is of coiled wire couched in a pattern of curving lines.

were usually placed at the top, with a fishpond at the lower edge. The figures were placed at either side of the mirror and were surrounded by flowers, birds, fruits and insects. An animal such as a lion, unicorn, leopard or camel would often be placed in each corner.

The more ornate frames had scalloped edges with a half-circle shape at the top and bottom. The corners were either squared or rounded. In some frames the border was divided into small panels, and one such example in the Salisbury and Wiltshire Museum has a medallion at the top enclosing a portrait of Charles II and another at the bottom containing a portrait of his Queen, Catherine of Braganza. At each side there is a full-length portrait of the King and Queen, and above them are motifs of flowers and leaves, while below the King is the lion of England and below the Queen the leopard of Braganza. The mirror is framed in imitation tortoiseshell and mounted on a rich dark-green velvet. It is thought to have been worked between 1660 and 1670.

At Cotehele House, near Callington, Cornwall, there is a very fine example with an immense amount of detailed stitching, which is in excellent condition. The frame has a scalloped edge and is quite large. The usual motifs are worked round the central mirror glass; tiny insects, birds on branches and an assortment of flowers fill any gaps between the larger motifs of figures, buildings and ponds. However, there is another mirror frame, not on show to the public, which has obviously not been so well cared for in the past and shows the ravages of time. Fortunately it has been rescued from complete dilapidation and is now kept under proper conditions. Although light, mildew and probably mice have all caused considerable damage, it is still a very interesting piece to study. Where the fabric and threads have worn away it is possible to examine the construction underneath, particularly of the figures. They seem to be built up from bundles of linen threads which have then been covered with fabric. In places the original design shows through, and although the drawing has a professional look, the actual needlework is quite amateur. It is certainly not as skilful as most of the embroidery of the period, and may have been the work of a younger and less experienced embroiderer. Half the appeal of historical embroidery lies in trying to visualize who did the stitching, where they lived and what their surroundings were like.

Another example of a complete mirror frame in the Victoria & Albert Museum is again rectangular in shape, and the borders are divided into small panels. In the centre at the top is a Nativity scene showing the Virgin Mary with the baby Jesus; Joseph stands behind her and the three wise men kneel at her feet. To the left is another Nativity scene in the stable, with oxen in the background. On the right-hand side are the shepherds with their sheep, and a small spotted dog, looking on. Beneath these panels are others containing an assortment of flowers and insects; below them are angels standing on chequered floors where a valiant attempt has been made at perspective. At the base of the frame the figure of a man (probably Joseph) leads a donkey on which are seated Mary and the baby. In the corners are a lion and a leopard, with birds sitting on branches just above them. Any spare space is, as usual, filled with beetles, snails, caterpillars and flowers.

It is fortunate that so many fine examples are still preserved, and the size and ornamentation provide clues to the status of the family to which the embroideress belonged. A very elaborate frame with scalloped edges, made of wood lacquered in the oriental style in black and gold must have come from a wealthy household.

Embroidered pictures

Numerous embroidered pictures worked during the seventeenth century still survive, some in pristine condition, with the colours still fresh and bright, but the majority, sadly, bearing the marks of time, where exposure to lights and the atmosphere have caused colours to fade and silks to perish. Sometimes bare spaces are left where once, small brilliant peacock feathers were applied. In the Elizabethan era, pictorial embroidery was very popular, and it was usually put to practical use, but in the seventeenth century, although the fashion for pictorial designs continued, they were used for more decorative purposes. Occasionally the embroideries would be used for elaborate cushions, but more often they were mounted as pictures and hung on the wall. The frames were constructed in real or imitation tortoiseshell, or in carved and lacquered wood.

Different techniques were used: some were

34 Picture, 1660, telling the story of Esther and Ahasueras. The two main characters are shown in the middle, with scenes from the story surrounding them. (*Victoria & Albert Museum, London*)

worked in tent stitch on a fine linen canvas, resembling a miniature tapestry; others were embroidered in long and short stitch on a satin background fabric. Occasionally the design would be worked entirely in beads, but the most popular method in mid-century was stumpwork, in which the principal motifs were raised from the surface. The subjects remained constant, being the same as those used for caskets and mirror frames. Biblical stories, the seasons, the Virtues, the liberal arts, the elements, and scenes from Ovid's *Metamorphoses* were all depicted over and over again. Many of the pictures tell a story almost in the manner of a present-day strip cartoon.

One such panel in the Victoria & Albert Museum is dated 1660, and tells the story of Esther and Ahasueras. In the centre, raised on a dais, sits the figure of Ahasueras beneath a canopy; in his hand is a sceptre which he is offering to Esther. She is shown attended by her two handmaidens, one of whom is holding up her cloak, while the other is shading her with a parasol held aloft. Both these figures are worked in flat stitches, in contrast to

35 Details from a panel in the Lady Lever Art Gallery, Port Sunlight, showing acorns and a fantastic beast. Both motifs are highly padded and covered with detached buttonhole stitch.

Esther who is richly dressed in the costume of the seventeenth century, parts of it raised and decorated with needlelace and tiny beads. At the top left of the picture is a gruesome scene of a man hanging from a gibbet, obviously Haman who was hanged for plotting. At the top right-hand side Esther's kinsman Mordecai stands at the castle gate. Along the top are two figures on horseback attended by their grooms, and in the background are another castle and some trees. In the bottom left-hand corner Esther entertains Ahasueras and Haman at a banquet. An elaborate fountain stands next to them, surrounded by ornamental rocks, on the right of which a large parrot with a surprised expression is seated on a branch. In the other corner a figure kneels beside a canopied bed on which lies Ahasueras. Any remaining spaces are filled with flowers, insects and animals. One wonders where the embroideress began: perhaps

the fascinating doll-like figures were assembled and applied first with the background stitchery left until last. This could be the reason why some embroideries are unfinished; perhaps when all the interesting pieces had been done enthusiasm ran out.

Not all the pictures were so crowded with incident; one in the Lady Lever Art Gallery at Port Sunlight shows the overthrow of Pharaoh and his host in the Red Sea, and is most realistic, without any of the characteristic additional motifs of flowers or insects (see figs 17, 35). It may be that it was the work of a more mature needlewoman.

Apart from the story panels, portraits, too, were popular. After the Restoration, Charles II was often depicted in raised work, and there is also a portrait of James II, dated 1686, the year of his coronation. The subjects of the portraits were sometimes members of the embroiderer's family. The actual head and shoulders were often worked in flat stitchery and contained within a highly raised border or cartouche, with further decoration in the four outside corners. A panel in the Victoria & Albert Museum is worked in silk on

36 A portrait of a lady in flat stitchery, surrounded by an oval frame raised from the background. At each corner there is the head of an angel in padded and raised embroidery. (*Victoria & Albert Museum, London*)

37 A portrait, said to be of Elizabeth Coombe. The head is worked in flat stitchery, and is contained within an elaborately raised frame, with an angel at each side. Flowers and animals complete the design. (*Embroiderers' Guild Collection*)

satin, using long and short stitch. A pastoral scene is shown in the background, with a shepherd and shepherdess tending their sheep. The medallion framing the portrait is edged with padded satin braid couched with silk and decorated with metal purlings. An angel's head in raised work and needlelace is worked in each corner.

A very similar piece is in the collection of the Embroiderers' Guild at Hampton Court, and is said to be a portrait of Elizabeth Coombe, who was herself an accomplished needlewoman. Again, the head and shoulders are embroidered in long and short stitch and the surrounding border is an elaborate oval, the foundation of which is a coil of linen threads couched into place with linen thread; over this is a further decoration of braid made from strips of vellum closely wrapped with silk thread and formed into loops. A finely coiled wire also covered with silk completes the border. Angels with rather sour expressions surround the oval frame; an outer frame, highly raised and also made from vellum, encloses them. Flowers in long and short stitch cover the remaining area, apart from the two bottom corners where on one side there is a lion and on the other a leopard. Both these animals are very highly padded. Although this picture has suffered the ravages of time, it nevertheless provides an interesting insight into the methods of working, and in consequence is of real value to the student of embroidery.

In the Fitzwilliam Museum in Cambridge another portrait shows the head and shoulders of a young woman, but in this case the head is padded and the features are painted on to the silk. The hair is not embroidered but fashioned from real hair, with some added coils of covered wire. Round the woman's neck is a circlet of seed pearls and tiny corals. She wears a bodice of figured silk which is

38 (*Top*) A detail from the portrait of Elizabeth Coombe, showing one of the angels. The head is padded and the features are embroidered on the covering fabric.

39 Another detail from the portrait, showing part of the border decoration made from silk-covered strips of vellum, and metal braid.

embroidered in satin stitch. The neck is trimmed with fine lace and further drapery is worked in needlepoint lace. The portrait is surrounded by flowers and animals, and in the background a country landscape can be seen, complete with the usual castle.

Some of the pictures which still exist are left unmounted, with the raw edges showing evidence of where they were stretched on to a frame for working. It may be that they belonged to sets of panels destined to be made up into caskets – yet more unfinished projects.

5
Methods for contemporary work

Planning an embroidery

A small sketchbook which can double as a notebook is as essential to the embroiderer as a needle and thread, so make a habit of jotting down ideas with colour notes and thoughts on fabrics and threads, stitches and methods of working. The drawings can be kept quite simple or be merely diagrams for future reference. Try to collect ideas and information with the same enthusiasm as you collect fabrics and threads.

The intricate appearance of stumpwork can all too easily appear fussy if the design is too complicated, or if too many different stitches and methods are used in one embroidery. It is best to plan a piece carefully and aim for a contemporary look, for there is no value in copying slavishly from the past. By all means adapt the stitches and the techniques of the seventeenth century, but be selective, and let the work reflect the age we live in.

It is preferable to work within a limited colour scheme; in fact, monochrome can be most effective for raised work, especially if different types and thicknesses of thread are used. The shadows cast by the padded areas will also alter the tones. Since stumpwork resembles low relief sculpture or carving, it is important to have a contrast between flat areas, slightly raised ones, and more highly padded ones. The tactile quality can be exploited; think of the beautiful carvings of Grinling Gibbons.

Obviously, when the design has been decided, the fabrics and threads have to be selected. Choose a firm weave for the background material; a smooth natural fibre is best, such as silk, cotton or fine wool. The background must be able to support the weight of applied fabrics and any embroidered 'slips'. A fine fabric should be mounted on to a fine cotton to give it more 'body', otherwise it will have a tendency to become puckered.

Transfer your design on to the background material, which should be mounted in a frame. This is especially important for raised work, as it will prevent the padded areas from being crushed. It will also be easier to work any surface stitchery before applying slips and padded motifs. Figures can be assembled separately before being stitched into place, although this will depend on the method chosen for their construction. The main consideration is to avoid rubbing the stitching and crushing any delicate pieces that have been applied. The design can be tacked on to the background with fine sewing cotton, or transferred directly by drawing on to the background with a water-soluble fibre-tipped pen.

The embroidery of the blackberries (fig. 43) shows how the work was planned from the beginning. Drawings were made of the flowers and berries in the summer, and at the same time a photograph was taken to act as a reference or memory-jogger when the berries had been eaten and the bramble pruned. To portray blackberries

40 (*Top*) A selection of materials used in contemporary stumpwork, including two thicknesses of wire, animal wool, modelling clay, balsa wood, fine canvas, vilene (pellon), stranded cotton and *coton à broder*.

41 Blackberries can provide a source of design for a small embroidery.

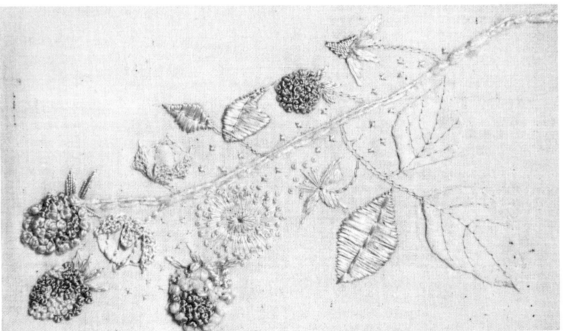

42 (*Top*) A drawing made from blackberries growing in a garden. Making a drawing allows you to be more selective than the camera, which is unable to cut out any unnecessary details.

43 An interpretation of the blackberries in embroidery, worked on fine calico in tones of white and cream, using silk threads. The stitches include detached buttonhole, satin stitch and french knots. Some of the berries are worked as separate slips and applied to the background.

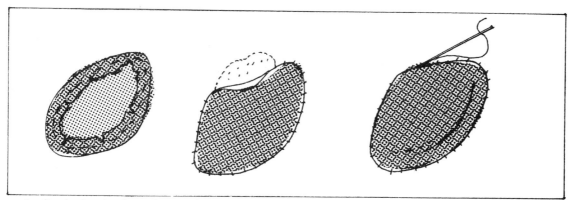

44 Appliqué, showing how the motif is cut out and applied to the background.

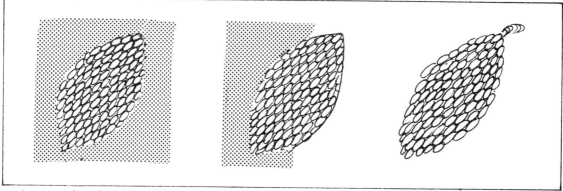

45 A canvas slip which is worked separately and then applied to the background.

46 An embroidery of leaves and berries. Some flowers and small leaves are worked in detached buttonhole stitch and the larger leaves are worked as canvas slips and applied to the silk background. The small berries are padded with vilene (pellon).

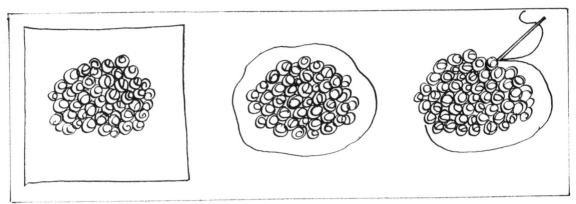

47 A calico slip worked in french knots and applied to the background.

in tones of white and cream may seem incongruous, but by keeping to a monochromatic colour scheme a complicated subject was translated into a simple design. If the leaves and berries had been embroidered in their natural colours the finished result might well have been too realistic, detracting from the contrast between the smooth leaves and the textured berries. The round knobbly shapes of the berries seemed well suited to french knots. Some were stitched directly on to the background and others were worked as separate slips which were then applied. Various thicknesses of silk thread were used for the stitching, and the slight sheen provided a foil to the matt surface of the fine calico used for the background.

Some of the leaves are embroidered in satin stitch and some in detached buttonhole, while others have been cut out in calico and applied to the background with tiny slip stitches, the raw edges being stroked underneath with the needle.

Stumpwork should be kept quite small; it is not a medium which lends itself to large-scale work, and stitches and threads should be correspondingly scaled down. If beads are used in the embroidery they should be quite tiny, any fabrics to be applied must be fine, and leather should be a soft suede or thin kid. The finished embroidery must be carefully mounted; if it is for a panel that is to be glazed, choose a clear picture glass, and allow space to accommodate the raised areas so that they are not flattened by any pressure.

The examples worked by contemporary embroiderers shown in this book are all mounted quite simply, and in most cases left unglazed.

METHODS

Appliqué

The shape of the motif can be drawn lightly on to the fabric, taking care to allow a margin for turning under. Remember to cut the shape on the straight grain of the fabric; if cut on the cross it will pucker when applied to the background material. This always has to be borne in mind when attaching one fabric to another; the grains should match for the best result.

Fold under the raw edges and hold in place with a few tacking stitches which can easily be removed later. Sew the motif in position using small slip stitches, and if it is going to be padded leave a gap so that the padding of animal wool can be inserted. Use a stiletto or a small knitting needle to push the wool gently into place. Close the gap with tiny stitches.

Canvas slips

It is advisable to use a fine canvas for work on such a small scale; eighteen holes to the inch or even finer will be suitable. A fine tailoring canvas, of the

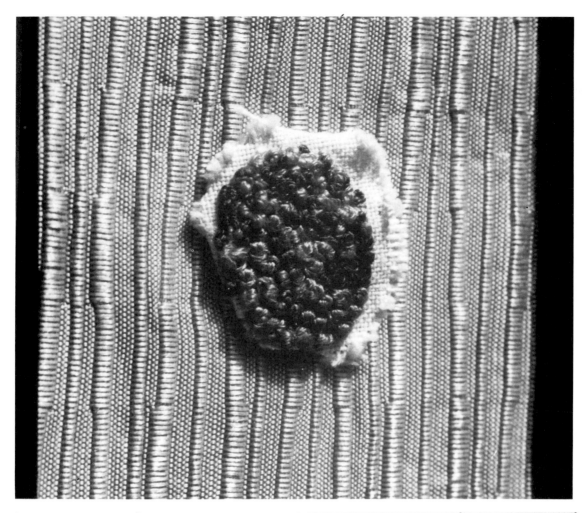

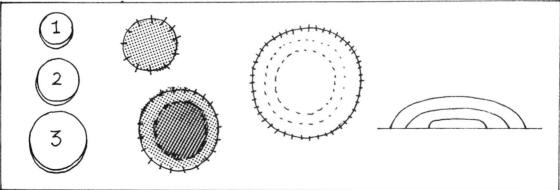

48 (*Top*) A slip of french knots worked on calico, cut out and applied to the background. The slip is stitched into place and the surplus calico tucked underneath.

49 Padding with three layers of felt graduated in size.

kind normally used for stiffening garments, is satisfactory to work on providing you have keen eyesight or a good magnifying glass!

Draw the motif on to the canvas (it is possible to use a soft pencil) and work the shape in simple canvas work stitches such as tent, gobelin, cross or hungarian. Anything too complex will be difficult to embroider on this scale. Try using different threads, contrasting matt with shiny; crewel wool, silk and stranded cotton are all suitable.

When the motif is complete, cut it out leaving a narrow edge all round. Fold this under carefully and slip stitch the shape on to the background material using a matching thread. Animal wool can be inserted if a highly raised effect is required. Traditionally, slips were finished by couching a fine cord around the outer edge, but this is unnecessary in contemporary work.

Calico slips

If a different texture is required, a slip can be worked on calico, cut out and applied in the same way as a canvas one. For the best result choose a medium-weight calico, draw the shape on to it, and fill the area completely with either french knots or bullion knots. Pack them densely together using a variety of threads in different thicknesses, and again contrast matt with shiny threads. Small beads can be interspersed with the knots to give a hint of sparkle. When the shape is entirely covered, cut out the motif leaving a narrow border (about one-eighth of an inch) to tuck under. Apply the slip to the background material in the same way as before, using extra padding if necessary, although knots so closely packed should provide enough height.

Padding

Many different materials can be used for padding to give a raised effect. A soft animal wool is best for padding applied shapes, whether they are fabric, or canvas or calico slips. The natural fibres compress more easily, giving a rounded shape – avoid using cotton wool, which will go lumpy and hard. Animal wool can be bought in small packets from the chemist or from craft shops which sell weaving materials, and only a small amount is needed as it goes a very long way.

TO PAD WITH FELT

Cut out the shape required, then a second one slightly smaller, and a third one smaller still. Sew these down in position one at a time, beginning with the smallest. Cover this one with the next size, and finally apply the largest shape over the previous two. Each piece of felt should be sewn down with tiny stab stitches, evenly spaced. Bring the thread up through the background material and down through the felt; this will prevent the felt from tearing. This method of padding gives a smooth, domed shape which can be covered either with a fine fabric or with thin kid. Stitches such as satin or detached buttonhole can be an alternative covering.

TO PAD WITH THICK VILENE

A thick vilene (pellon), normally used in furnishings, can be used instead of felt, and this will give a flatter, crisper look and provide a contrast to the softer appearance of felt. A difference in the height of the raised areas will create a more interesting embroidery. Draw out the shape required and cut out the vilene to the exact size, on this occasion. Use two tacking stitches to hold it in position on the background material, and then closely cover the shape with satin stitches, taking the stitches over and over. Two strands of a stranded cotton will give a good result; be careful to lay the threads side by side to obtain a smooth finish. You may find it helps to begin at the middle of the shape and work outwards, first one way and then the other. This makes it easier to control the stitches at the ends of the motif. A variegated thread can look most effective with this method. Thick vilene can also be covered with fine fabric before it is applied to the background. Cut the fabric out slightly larger than the vilene shape and tuck the turnings

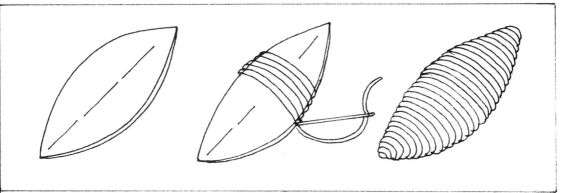

50 (*Top*) A detail showing how the segments of a pineapple have been worked by padding with felt, which has been covered with thin silk and gold kid. Each segment is stitched in place with fly stitch or eyelet stitch.

51 Padding with a thick vilene (pellon) to raise an area slightly.

over the edges, securing them with a few tacking stitches; sew down on the background with tiny slip stitches. These smooth shapes contrast well with slips of french knots.

Stiffening shapes with wire

Shapes which stand away from the background can be worked over a foundation of wire. Fine craft wire or fine florist's wire are the most suitable, as they are pliable yet firm enough to hold their shape. The wire should be cut to the required length and then closely covered with thread. A soft thread such as a stranded cotton is the easiest to use; a springy silk or wool will be difficult to wrap with and the finished result will be disappointing. Take one or two threads of the stranded cotton, and cut a length about three times as long as the wire. Tie the thread on to one end of the wire, and begin wrapping. To prevent the thread from slipping, bend the tip of the wire over to hold the knot in place. Wrap very carefully and tightly until all the wire is covered, then fasten off securely with another knot. The wire can then be shaped by bringing the two ends together and twisting them round each other. The shape is now ready to be filled with needlelace stitches; detached button-hole is a good stitch to begin with, as it is quite simple to do. Other more complicated stitches can be used when you have had more practice. Take a fine single thread, either *coton à broder* or fine crochet cotton, and tie a length on to the twisted end of the wire. Using the wire as an anchorage, work buttonhole stitches along one half of the shape, then work backwards to the beginning, working into the loops of the previous stitches. When you reach the twisted ends, work a stitch round the wire, and then buttonhole along into the second row of loops. Carry on working in this way, back and forth, until the shape is filled; at the final row work the stitches round the wire to keep them secure. At the beginning of each row check that you have enough thread for the return journey, but if you do run out of thread, weave it in carefully. When you are working the stitches, either pin the

52 Padding with thick vilene (pellon). The motif is tacked into position and close satin stitch is worked over the top. The finished result is smooth, even, and slightly raised from the surface.

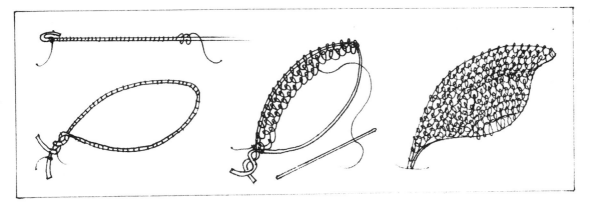

53 (*Top*) Covering fine wire to make a stiffened motif which will stand away from the surface.

54 The inside of a box lid, showing a trellis covered with leaves and climbing stems. The trellis is made from wooden cocktail sticks bound with thread, the stems and tendrils are fashioned from wrapped wire, and the leaves are worked in detached buttonhole stitch. (*Margaret Rivers*)

shape to the side of the embroidery frame, which will leave both hands free, or hold the shape in one hand and work the stitches with the other. It is for you to decide which you find easiest. The completed shape can be attached to the background by making a small hole in the material with either a stiletto or a large tapestry needle, through which the twisted ends of the wire can be posted, and secured on the back with small stitches. In seventeenth-century embroideries, groups of petals and leaves were worked in this way.

Making purling

It is difficult to make a covered wire exactly like that which was used in the seventeenth century, but a similar effect can be achieved with some skill – and a good deal of patience! Use a very fine copper craft wire and cut a piece which is three times as long as the finished length required. Take a fine thread, tie it on to one end of the wire and wrap it round tightly and closely, knotting it securely at the finishing end. Now wind this covered wire tightly round a large darning needle and slide it off very carefully; the result should be a small coil resembling a watch spring. The coil can be sewn in place either by threading a needle through the coil, or by couching it down between the coils. This is similar to using the stiff pearl purl in goldwork. Unfortunately only short lengths can be made by this method, but they are effective for certain areas.

Unstiffened lacy shapes

A softer motif can be worked which is similar to needlemade lace in appearance. Use a fine muslin or thin vilene interfacing as a foundation for the stitching, mounted in a small ring frame. Draw out the motif to be worked and oversew a firm thread round the edge, covering it closely to give the effect of a fine cord. The method is similar to 'trailing' in whitework, and serves the same purpose as a cordonnet in lace making. Work a lacy filling

within the shape; this could be detached buttonhole, hollie point, treble brussels, or corded filling. Keep all the stitching on the surface, using the 'cord' edging to anchor the thread. A fine thread is essential, and a fine crochet cotton, number seventy or finer, will be ideal. When the motif is finished, cut it away from the foundation very carefully, using a pair of small scissors with good, sharp points. Keep as close to the stitching as possible but make sure none of the stitches are cut; turn the motif over and cut away the fabric from the back. It is now ready to be stitched on to the background of the embroidery. Attach the motif at one end only so that it will stand away from the background.

Wrapping vellum

It is possible to buy sheets of vellum from any good art and craft supplier who sells equipment for calligraphers. A good-quality cartridge paper can be substituted if vellum is not obtainable, although it does not stand up to handling as well. Cut a narrow strip of vellum to the length required and wrap it closely with thread; stranded cotton or silk work well. To begin, lay a short piece of the thread along the vellum and wrap back to cover the end; carry on wrapping firmly until the whole strip is covered, then thread the end of the cotton or silk back through the wrapping a short way to secure the end. This can be done easily with a tapestry needle. The vellum strip can now be used in the same way as a stiff ribbon or braid, and when couched into folds or a pattern of loops it makes an effective border or frame.

Raised stems and borders

Straight borders or curving stems can both be made from a foundation of linen or similar firm threads gathered into a bundle or skein and couched into position. Space the couching stitches evenly about one eighth of an inch apart and, using these stitches as a ladder, work raised stem band

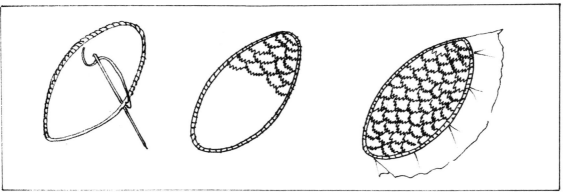

55 A lacy motif which can be worked separately before being applied to the background.

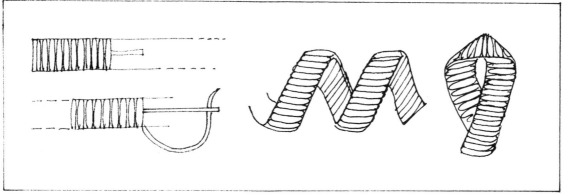

56 Wrapping a thin strip of vellum with thread.

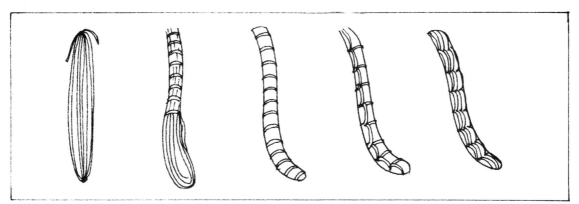

57 Making raised stems or bands by laying down bundles of thread and covering them with raised stem band stitch.

stitch over the top. Work down one length, then go
back to the beginning and work the next row;
repeat this process until the foundation of linen
threads is completely covered. This method is used
in Casalguidi work, and gives a raised line which is
rounded and well suited to making curving lines
and turning corners. Another way to make a
corded line is to take a length of string, wrap it
closely (in the same way as vellum), and stitch it in
position. This will give a thinner harder line, and
provides another variation. Narrow strips of thick
vilene (pellon) can be tacked in place and then
covered with satin stitch to make flatter borders or
structures.

58 A small bag in Casalguidi work, showing the use of
raised areas and detached buttonhole stitch. (*Embroiderers' Guild Collection*)
59 Another example of Casalguidi work, showing the
elaborate tassels which often decorated the small bags.
(*Embroiderers' Guild Collection*)

60 A small square box made of wood with a padded and
embroidered top. Narrow strips of fine kid are ruched
and couched into place, and some grapes are also made
from kid, while others are padded and covered with
detached buttonhole stitch. The leaves are wired and
filled with detached buttonhole stitch.

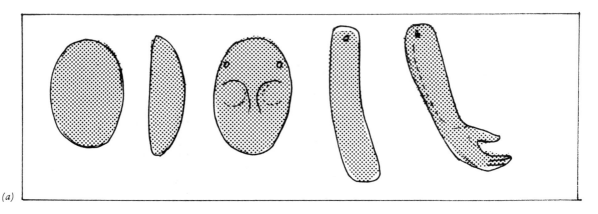

(a)

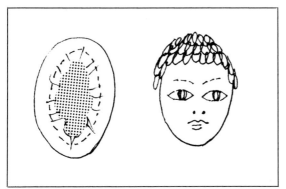

(b)

61 (a) & (b) Using modelling clay to make heads and hands. The heads may then be covered with fine fabric before adding the features.

Modelling clay

Modelling clay makes a good substitute for the wooden moulds that were used in seventeenth-century work. There are many different types of clay available, and they often come in a range of colours. Some clays are made to dry on contact with the air; others need to be hardened in the oven for a short time at a low temperature. Full instructions are given on the packets. The type which needs to be hardened is often easier to use, as it is more pliable and will not crack from the heat of the hands when manipulated. When the clay is to be used for modelling faces and hands, it is an advantage if it is a flesh colour which will not need to be painted when it has dried. And clay which is to be used for making fruit, for instance, would be

best in a colour to match the motif, especially if it is to be covered with stitching, where small gaps may occur. Before the clay dries, make one or two small holes in the mould with a large needle so that it can be attached to the background in the same way as a bead. When modelling a head for a figure do not attempt to be too realistic; suggest the features quite simply. For example, two small hollows for the eye sockets will be sufficient. Make an oval shape, and mark the eyes half-way down to make the proportion visually correct, keeping the back of the mould flat and smooth so that it will be close to the background when it is finished. The head could either have the features painted on, or be covered with fine fabric and then the details embroidered on quite simply. Fruits, animals' heads, or any small object can be modelled from clay and covered with either stitches or fabric. The fabric needs to be cut out to a similar shape, but allowing plenty of extra material which can be gathered up with a thread run round the edge. It can then be placed over the mould and secured, ready to be sewn in position with tiny slip stitches.

Assembling figures

There are various ways in which figures can be fashioned, and the embroiderer should adopt a method that is suited to the design. One way is to construct the figure on a separate piece of fabric and then cut it out and apply it to the background. Leave a narrow edge all round, which can be

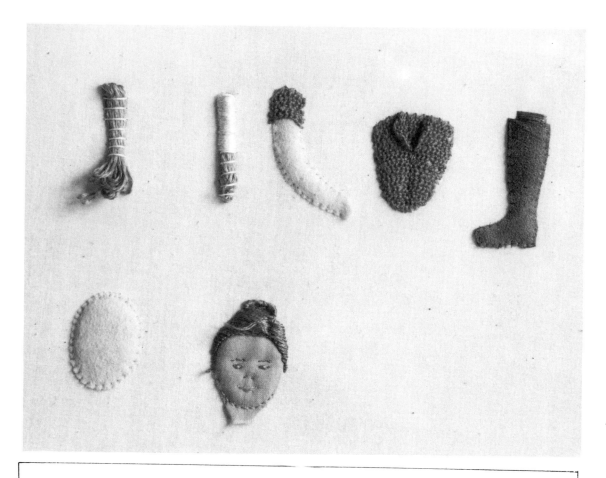

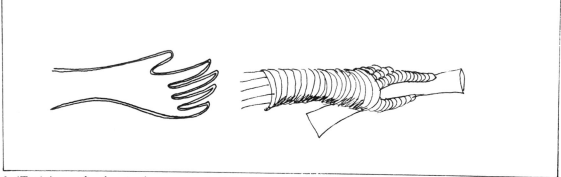

62 (*Top*) A sampler showing how to start building up a figure. Linen threads are stitched in position and covered with satin stitch. Padded felt is covered either with fabric, fine kid, or detached buttonhole stitch. The head is constructed from three graded layers of felt, which are then covered with fabric and the features embroidered on top.

63 Hands made from wrapping fine wire with thread. The fingers are then shaped to the desired position, and can be made to clasp small objects.

64 Figures climbing a tree. The heads and hands of the two figures are made from modelling clay, and the bodies from padded felt covered with fabric. (*Valerie Thomas*)

folded under in the same way as when applying a slip. In the seventeenth century the figures were often assembled in this way and then glued to thin card before being stitched in place. Alternatively, the figure can be built up directly on to the final piece of embroidery. In either case, the ways of constructing the figure will be much the same. First of all the figure should be drawn out carefully on paper, taking care to make a pleasing shape and bearing in mind the proportions. Trace the figure on the backing fabric, which should be firmly mounted in a frame for ease of working. Begin by building up the body, arms and legs: this can be done by layering felt as already described, or by laying down bundles of linen or firm thread which are then carefully couched into place. The hands and feet can be stitched in position next; hands can either be modelled from clay or fashioned from covered wire, which is bent to form the palm and fingers. Again, choose the method which is best suited to the figure; if the hands are to grasp something then the wire framework is the most suitable construction. The feet, too, can be of modelling clay or merely padded felt covered with fine kid. Now the figure is ready for the head to be placed in position. This can be built up from layers of felt and then covered with fine fabric on to which the features are embroidered, or alternatively can be modelled in clay, as previously described. The final details of the clothing and hair are determined by the type of figure being portrayed.

Detached buttonhole is the most versatile stitch for covering the body and limbs, and can give the appearance of knitted fabric. Satin stitch is also very useful for covering areas, or small scraps of fabric can be used. The hair can be fashioned from threads looped and stitched into shape, or perhaps made from french knots or bullion knots. Detached buttonhole stitch worked just over the top of the modelled head is often a useful way of giving an anchorage for more elaborate stitching. Re-

65 'A Pop Singer'. The head is made from a wooden bead. The hands and feet are constructed from wire bound with thread, and the clothes are hand-knitted in a fine thread. (*Susan Fielding*)

member to keep all fabrics and threads in scale to the small size of the figure, and any other form of decoration such as beads should also be kept quite small. Figures in action are the most interesting, and the figures may be naturalistic or stylized, depending on the result required. Try not to copy them from embroideries of the past, but give them the look of today.

These are the basic methods which can be used in contemporary stumpwork, but the embroiderer will discover for herself other ways of working and making raised areas; anything which gives the desired result is permissible, so long as the scale is borne in mind.

6
Learning stitches

Apart from the stitches used in traditional stumpwork, there are many others which give a raised effect when worked, and it is worth looking through the reference books to find the more unusual ones. Nowadays, embroiderers often use only one or two different stitches in their work, french knots and straight stitches being amongst the most popular. This is fine if it produces the desired effect, but it can be monotonous; raised work provides an excuse, if one is needed, for trying out a wider vocabulary of stitches.

To give variety to an embroidery, it is a good idea to contrast flat surface stitches with raised ones. Satin stitch, for example, can be worked in both ways, either lying flat or raised from the surface by padding. Laid threads couched with another colour can be arranged in patterns, and, like satin stitch, the play of light will change according to the direction in which the stitches are worked. Seeding or speckling will give a different texture from french knots and can be worked in various densities to give the appearance of shading.

When you are learning a new stitch, work it in the traditional way and then experiment by altering the scale and direction of stitching. Try using different types of thread, some thin and some thick; this will make a considerable difference to the look of most stitches, and you will discover which thread produces the result you require. Before beginning a piece of embroidery it is worth while to learn some new stitches which will be useful in raised work.

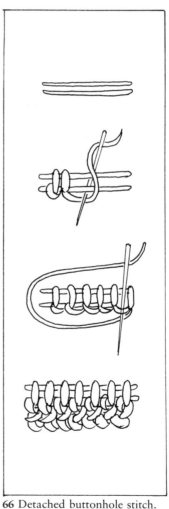

66 Detached buttonhole stitch.

67 An example of detached buttonhole stitch worked as free-standing shapes, attached to the background only at the top.

Detached buttonhole stitch

Of all the stitches used in stumpwork, detached buttonhole is probably the most useful. Begin by making a bar of two long stitches about 2 cm (¾ in.) in length, laid closely together one below the other. Starting at one end, work ordinary buttonhole stitches over the bar without taking the needle through the fabric. The stitches should be kept quite close together, but avoid pulling them too tightly. When the bar is covered, take the needle through to the back of the fabric and bring it up just below, ready to work the next row using the loops of the previous row as an anchorage. When this second row is complete, take the needle to the back of the work again and up just below, ready to begin the third journey. Work backwards and forwards in this way until the area to be covered is filled, and then take the needle through to the back and fasten off. The whole area should be detached from the background fabric, except for the sides. A tapestry needle is recommended for this stitch, and a firm thread such as *coton à broder* or a crochet cotton will give the best result.

A row of five or six back stitches can be used as an alternative foundation, and in this case the first row is worked into the back stitches. Make two buttonhole stitches into each back stitch and then proceed as before.

68 Detached buttonhole stitch used in a free way on the walls of a building, combined with padded areas. (*Patricia Broughall*)

Ceylon stitch

In some ways this is similar to detached buttonhole, as the stitches are attached at the sides only, with the finished result resembling knitting. Start by making a long stitch of about 2 cm (¾ in.) in length, and on this foundation work a row of loops. Take the needle through to the back of the fabric when you reach the end, and bring it up a little way below ready to begin again. Work into the loops and continue back and forth until the area is complete. As you can see from the diagram, the action differs from buttonhole stitch.

Hollie stitch

This is a stitch used in making needlelace, sometimes known as 'holy point lace'. Like the two previous stitches, it is detached from the background fabric, apart from the edges. To make a foundation, work an outline of chain stitches round the shape to be covered. Bring the needle up through the end chain stitch at the top right, then take the thread across to the other side and insert the needle through to the back; bring it up in the middle of the chain stitch below. Wind the thread round your thumb from right to left and pass the

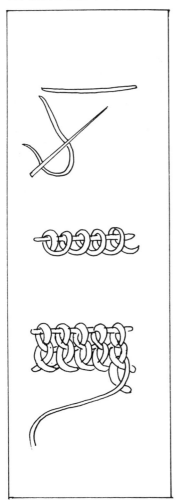

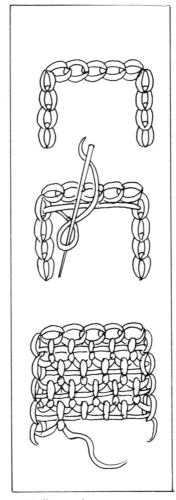

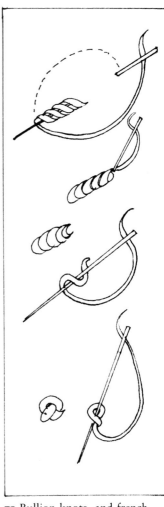

69 Ceylon stitch.

70 Hollie stitch.

71 Bullion knots, and french knots below.

needle through the chain stitch above, under the laid thread, and down through the loop which is round the thumb. By this action the thread is made secure, as shown in the diagram. Work along the row in this way and at the end take another thread across as before, and continue working until the area is covered. Each time the thread is taken through the chain stitch, under the laid thread and down through the loop on the thumb.

Bullion knots

Bullion knots are sometimes called 'caterpillar stitch' or 'coil stitch'. They are a useful way of adding texture, particularly as they can be worked in a variety of threads from silks to wools. A thick needle with a narrow eye is the most suitable to use; choose a thread of medium thickness for practising. Work the knots either as a filling or as a curving line. Fasten on the thread, bring the needle out and insert it again a short distance away (to make the length of knot), but bring out only the tip of the needle. Twist the thread round the tip five or six times, and then pull the needle through these twists very carefully; secure the knot by inserting the needle into the original hole. A stitch known as 'Porto Rico rose' can be made by working bullion knots arranged in a coil to form a small flower.

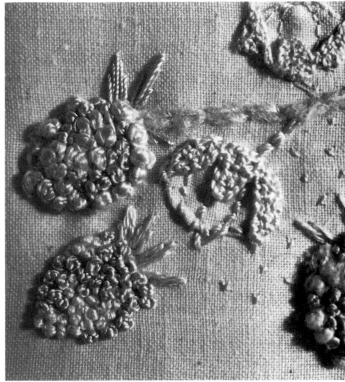

72 Berries made from densely stitched french knots in different thicknesses of thread. Some are worked directly on to the background and others are applied in the form of slips.

French knots

These are also useful in providing areas of texture and although they can be worked singly, they are more effective when they are grouped closely together. To begin, fasten on the thread and bring the needle out, hold the thread tightly and twist it once round the needle, which is then taken through to the back of the fabric very close to the starting point. Pull the needle through carefully, leaving a dimpled knot on the surface. For extra variety, use different weights of thread and contrast matt with shiny.

Padded satin stitch

The finished look of this stitch depends on its having a neat foundation. To make the required shape, work a basis of short straight parallel stitches, lying close together; over these sew long stitches side by side in the opposite direction to cover the area and give a smooth finish. This final layer of stitches can be worked either straight or slanting. Take the thread right over the back of the fabric so that there is as much on the underneath as there is on the surface. Working closely and evenly will ensure that you have a firm, neat edge to the finished shape.

Picots

There are a number of different ways of working picots, but the most useful for raised work is the woven picot. For this stitch, choose a firm thread and begin by making a loop on top of the fabric, then insert a pin over the loop and into the fabric. The threaded needle is now passed behind the head of the pin and woven to and fro through the loop until it is filled. Fasten off the thread and remove the pin. Keep the stitches as even as possible. Small picots worked in overlapping rows can look very effective.

73 A florist's shop with buckets outside, filled with brightly coloured flowers, could provide inspiration for an embroidery. (*Kate Turnbull*)
74 Bunches of sweet williams in bright pinks and reds are all stitched in french knots, some of which are worked as separate slips and applied to the background. (*Mary Fortune*)

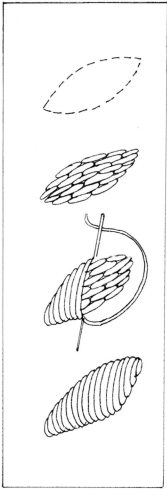

75 Padded satin stitch.

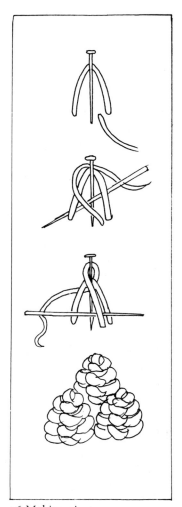

76 Making picots.

Seeding

This stitch is also known as 'speckling', and both words are descriptive of the effect it gives on the surface. Almost any thread is suitable, and by using tones of one colour it is possible to create an effect of shading by merging the tones together. Tiny stitches are worked at all angles and can be stitched quite densely then gradually spaced out to give the appearance of having been swept together. Seeding is useful for working as a background to voided shapes, or as a filling where french knots might be too heavy.

Raised cup stitch

A firm thread such as *coton à broder* is best for this stitch, and it will be easier to work if a tapestry needle is used. Make a small triangle of stitches approximately $\frac{1}{2}$ cm ($\frac{1}{4}$ in.) in length, and on to this framework make buttonhole stitches, working round the three sides of the triangle. Continue round and round until a cup is formed, then weave the thread down through the stitches and fasten off. A variation can be made by gradually decreasing the number of buttonhole stitches so that the finished result is closed up to a point.

77 A detail of picots densely packed together to form the leaves of a tree. (*Barbara Dunhill*)

1. The top of a casket showing the figures of King Charles I and Queen Henrietta Maria. The figures are raised and padded, and are shown standing in front of two castles with the sun shining above them. Their court clothes of the period are decorated with lace and seed pearls. *(On loan to the Dorset Natural History and Archaeological Society, Dorset County Museum, Dorchester)*

2. A detail from the casket in colour pl. 1, showing a fantastic bird with wings standing away from the background.

3. Another bird motif from the casket.

4. A side panel of the casket, showing two of the figures. This particular casket has been very well preserved, and consequently the colours remain remarkably bright and the stitching is in good condition.

5. A cabinet decorated with pastoral scenes and animals. English, 1650-1700. The background fabric is silk satin and the embroidery is in coloured silks and metal threads including purls. Some areas of the design are raised and padded. *(Burrell Collection, Glasgow Museums and Art Galleries)*

6. Mirror frame, a contemporary version of a stumpwork frame based on a design of various fruits. *(Barbara Dunhill)*

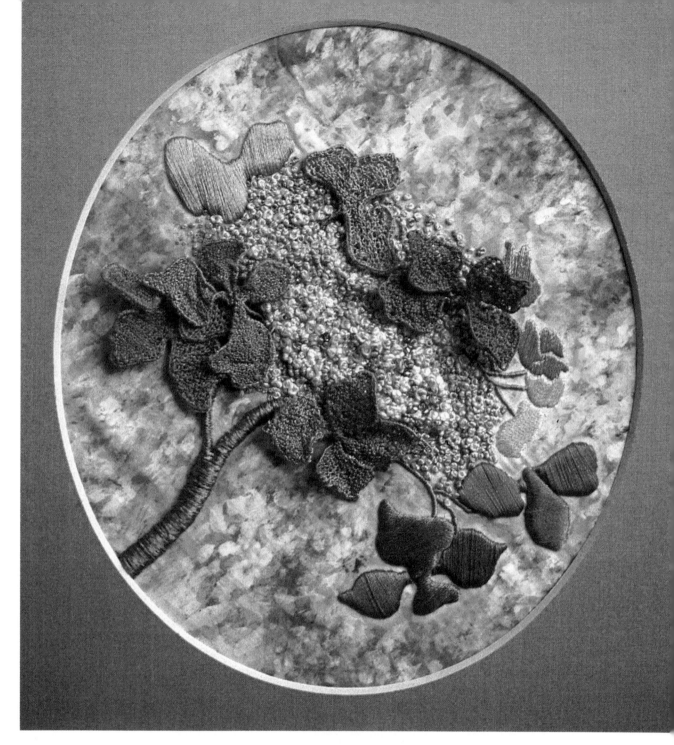

7. *Opposite* 'The Spencers Gardening', a scene reflecting everyday life. The two figures are both padded and raised from the background; the man is holding a spade, and the woman is bending to gather vegetables. *(Ann Sutton)*

8. 'Hydrangea'. This particular flower is always a favourite with embroiderers, and each one interprets it differently. The panel has a very textural quality with parts of the design heavily padded. Detached petals worked over a wire framework add to the three-dimensional effect. *(Christine Bloxham)*

9. 'The Collector', an embroidery which combines many different materials, objects and techniques. The box is constructed of hand-made bark paper and set on a wool background. The figure, made from wool, carries an assortment of objects of carved wood, copper and porcupine quill. *(Wilke Smith)*

10. 'Little Precious', a contemporary version of a casket which is purely decorative, telling the story of a fond family gazing at the new baby. (*Ann Rutherford*)

11. 'Sugared Almonds and Mixed Boilings'. Brightly coloured sweets in jars sit on a shelf. Fabric painting is combined with surface stitchery and raised work in this panel. (*Vicky Lugg*)

12. 'Apples on a Check Cloth', a panel which combines goldwork with surface stitchery, raised work and trapunto quilting.

13. 'Ice-cream Parlour'. Surface stitchery, trapunto quilting and raised work are combined in this panel.

78 A detail from a mirror frame showing berries and leaves. The berries are french knot slips, with the leaves stitched flat to the background. (*Barbara Dunhill*)

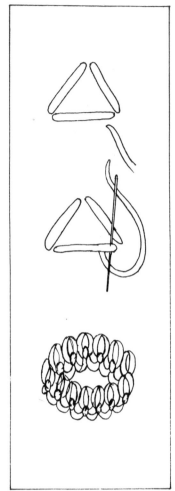

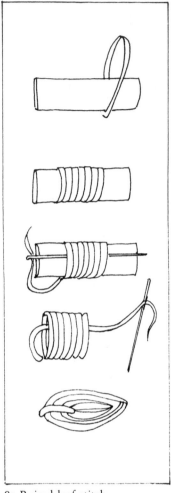

79 Seeding or speckling, showing how it can be used to void a shape.

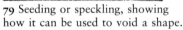

80 Raised cup stitch.

81 Raised leaf stitch.

Raised leaf stitch

To work this stitch, a narrow strip of card is needed to act as a template. Cut a piece about 0.3 cm ($\frac{1}{8}$ in.) wide and 2.5 cm (1 in.) long. Fasten on a length of stranded cotton, using four or six strands, and hold the strip of card on the fabric in an upright position. Now work six or seven stitches over the card and into the fabric, keeping them even and closely side by side; bring the needle up close to the last stitch and thread it through all the loops to the first one, remove the card very carefully and pull back the needle ready to insert it

again at the other end. The finished stitch should look like a small leaf which is slightly raised from the surface.

Banksia rose stitch

For the best result use a stranded cotton, either four or six strands according to the size required. Fasten on the thread and make a small loop an eighth of an inch in height. Work three more loops the same size and close together to form the centre

82 Banksia rose stitch.

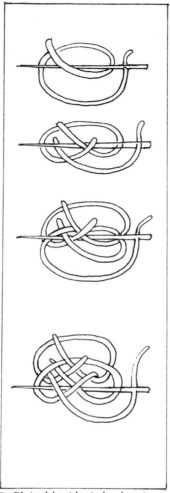

83 Plaited braid stitch, showing the sequence of working.

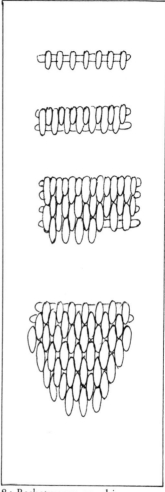

84 Basketweave couching.

of the rose. Take a small back stitch near to the loops to keep them secure; now work long stem stitches round the centre, leaving them as loose and high as the middle stitches. Four stem stitches should be enough to encircle the centre, continue working round in this way but gradually decrease the height of the stem stitches so that by the fourth row they should be almost flat to the surface. Take care to work the stitches close to each other so that the 'petals' appear to enfold one another. A variegated thread shading from dark to light is very effective. The secret is to get the tension right, and not to make the centre loops too big; it is worth

working slowly and carefully to get a good result. Banksia is the name of an old-fashioned rose, and this stitch was very popular as a decoration for both household linen and dress in the 1930s.

Curl stitch

Curl stitch gives the effect of a narrow cord, and can be worked in a straight line or a curving one. To begin, make a foundation of evenly spaced running stitches and work a second line back to fill in the gaps. Oversew these stitches closely to make a smooth corded line, keeping all the stitches on the surface without pulling the needle through the fabric. If an extra-thick line is needed, a row of buttonhole stitches can be worked over the cord, again without taking the needle through to the back.

Plaited braid stitch

This is an intricate stitch which makes a good decorative border or edging. It is necessary to work the stitch in a firm thread, otherwise the stitches will lose their shape. The method of working is best described in diagrams (see fig. 83), and you will see that the needle only goes through the fabric on alternate movements; at other times it is interlaced through the loops on the surface. When the needle is put through the fabric, take care to bring it out exactly beneath so that all the loops are in line. If the stitch is worked correctly there should be a row of horizontal stitches on the reverse of the fabric which are all the same length and evenly spaced. This stitch was popular in Elizabethan embroidery and was often worked in a metal thread.

These are just a few of the many interesting and more complex stitches which are useful for raised work, and a browse through an old embroidery book is always worth while to discover still more that may be seldom used. Even by studying old embroideries it is possible to work out how some of the unfamiliar stitches were worked. One such stitch frequently used in seventeenth-century embroidery does not appear in any of the reference books available today, so the correct name is not known, but 'basketweave couching' describes it quite well. It is a stitch best suited to working on canvas or an evenweave linen, but it can be used on other fabrics if care is taken with spacing. Begin by marking out the shape you require. Using a medium-weight thread, take a long stitch across the top of the shape, and over this work small straight stitches, leaving a space between each one just big enough to fill in with another stitch on the second row. Take another long stitch across immediately below the first row; work along with straight stitches over the bar and filling in the gaps. Repeat in the same way until the shape is filled. The finished stitching should look like basketwork, and the long stitches underneath will raise it slightly from the surface.

7
Making a sampler for reference

Before embarking on a finished piece of embroidery which includes stumpwork techniques, it is a good idea to make a sampler of stitches and methods. This can be used as a reference to help determine which techniques are best suited to the design. Too often it is tempting to begin with great enthusiasm, unaware of the pitfalls which can lead to disappointment with the finished result. It is better to learn at the outset which fabrics and threads are suitable for particular techniques and stitches. The latter worked in silk can look very different worked in stranded cotton or fine wool, and only one of these may give the desired effect.

For the sampler a plain cotton fabric such as calico is ideal to work on, as it is a firm weave of medium thickness which will take most threads easily and also support any applied fabrics and slips. It has the added advantage that notes can be written on to the material in pen or pencil alongside the actual stitches and methods. The sampler is purely for individual use, so how it is set out is for the embroiderer to decide: it does not have to be a work of art, but merely a reference.

For ease of working and to make sure all the important points are covered, the following exercises are set out stage by stage. First of all cut a piece of calico to fit a 20 cm (8 in.) ring frame. It is a good idea to bind the inner ring with a narrow tape, as this will help to keep the material taut while you work.

1 *Detached buttonhole stitch.* This versatile stitch was extensively used in the embroideries of the seventeenth century, and it is once again popular for contemporary raised work. The appearance of the stitch can be altered according to the thickness of the thread used and the size and tension of the stitches. Begin by mastering the basic stitch, and work five or six rows. Try to keep the tension even and avoid pulling the stitches too tightly. A single thread such as *coton à broder* or a crochet cotton of similar thickness will give the best result, and a tapestry needle will be best for working through the loops.

2 The next stage is to work a group of detached buttonhole stitches, each group overlapping the other, until an area of texture is made. Start by making a foundation of three back stitches; into each stitch work two buttonhole stitches, then without taking the needle through to the back of the work, continue stitching to and fro into the loops of the previous row. These picots can be shaped to a point or be rounded by missing a loop at each side in much the same way as decreasing in crochet. To finish off, weave the thread in and out along one side of the stitching, take it through to the back of the work and fasten off. Continue this process until you have several shapes close together, all of which are attached to the fabric by their foundation stitches only.

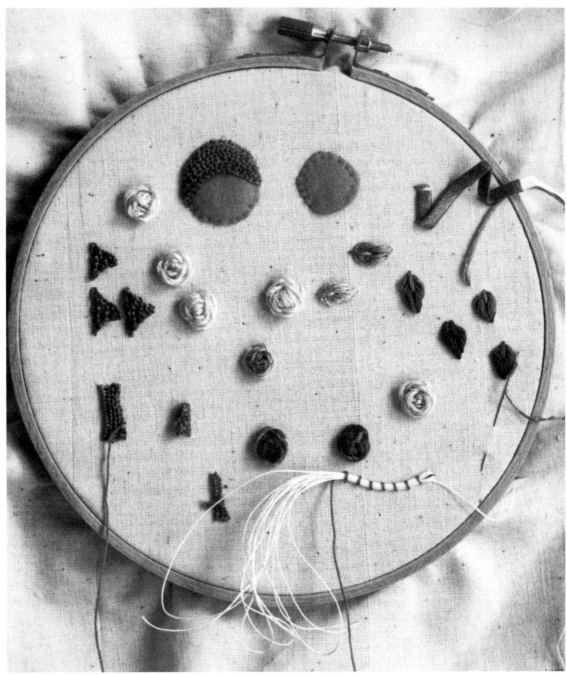

85 A sampler showing stitches and methods which include padding with felt, wrapped vellum, detached buttonhole stitch, raised leaf stitch and banksia rose stitch.

86 A sampler worked on calico, with notes written next to the stitches and methods to act as a reference. (*Betty Swadling*)
87 A finished embroidery based on a hydrangea, using some of the stitches and methods worked in the sampler. (*Betty Swadling*)

3 The third step is to make a small padded motif by layering pieces of felt in graduated sizes. For ease of working, make the shape either a circle, oval or rectangle; an irregular edge may prove difficult to cover with stitching. Fix the smallest shape in position using small stab stitches, then over this put the middle-sized one, stitching it down in the same way, and finally sew the largest shape over these two. This should give a smooth domed shape which can be covered with detached buttonhole stitch. It is well worth taking the time to sew each piece down separately; do not be tempted to take a short cut by

88 A detail showing sheep made by padding with felt which has been covered with detached buttonhole stitch using a fine wool thread. (*Barbara Dunhill*)

89 'Hellebore', a small embroidery in fine silk threads using detached buttonhole stitch and basketweave couching. (*Jennie Parry*)

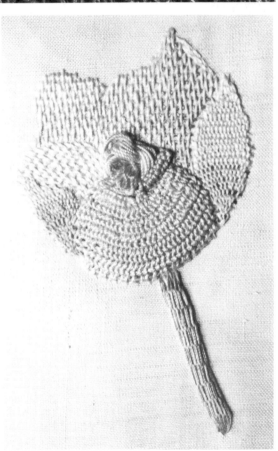

stitching them in place all together, for the result will be disappointing.

Start by making a foundation of small back stitches around one third of the shape, on the background fabric but close to the felt. Continue working back along the loops of these stitches, taking the needle through the calico only at the edge of the shape, and decreasing or increasing as necessary. Work as evenly as you can, and when the felt is covered take the stitches on the last row through to the back of the work. The whole covering of stitches will now be held firmly in place. The elasticity of detached buttonhole means that quite highly padded shapes can be covered successfully. On a finished project it is advisable to match the colour of the felt to the thread used for stitching. By this time you will have gained confidence in using this stitch, so why not try using a finer thread, which will give the appearance of lace.

90 A small box, showing the lid, which is decorated with padded insects. The bodies are made from felt covered with stitching, some of the wings are stiffened with wire, and others are shaped from vilene and covered with fabric. (*Jean Southwood*)

4 *Wired shapes.* Completely free-standing motifs can be made in detached buttonhole stitch over a framework of fine wire which has been closely covered with thread. (See Chapter 5.) Petals or leaf shapes are suitable for practising. Make each one separately, and apply them to the sampler by making a small hole with either a stiletto or a tapestry needle and putting the twisted ends of the wire shape through to the back of the work. Finish by securing with tiny stitches. The finished motif can then be bent into position. Try different filling stitches for the motifs, perhaps hollie stitch or any needlepoint filling. Stepped buttonhole bar will give a very lacy effect. The wire in fact provides the same type of basis as a cordonnet in needlemade lace.

91 A detail from a mirror frame showing two apples, one made as a canvas slip and the other worked in smooth satin stitch over thick vilene. (*Barbara Dunhill*)
92 'Cockerel'. The body of the bird is made from shapes of vilene (pellon) covered with satin stitch, and interspersed with french knots. The tail feathers are cut from fine suede. (*Carol Brailey*)

5 *Padded satin stitch*. In contrast to the textured look of detached buttonhole stitch, try covering a padded shape with close satin stitch. Cut a simple shape from thick vilene (pellon), place it on the background and hold it in position with two tacking stitches. Using two strands of stranded cotton, cover the shape with stitches; start from the middle and work outwards, taking care to get the thread to lie smoothly. Remember to take the thread right over the back of the work, as working over and over will give a better finish. There should be as much thread on the back of the work as on the front, and it will help if the needle is angled slightly as it goes in and out. When you have completed one half, go back to the middle and work the rest. Working

93 (*Top*) A drawing of trees for a small embroidery to be worked in french knots on calico and then applied in the form of slips.

94 An embroidery based on a drawing of a group of trees. French knot slips have been applied to the background, and some of the slips have been padded with animal wool to give extra height. Other details have been stitched directly on to the background.

in this way it is easier to control the stitches at each end. Different tones of thread can be used, and variegated stranded cotton is very effective too.

Of course, padded satin stitch can be worked in the traditional way over a foundation of stitches laid in the opposite direction to the covering ones, but it is sometimes difficult to get a really smooth finish. However, using the thick vilene as a base ensures a painless, crisp finish each time.

6 *French knot slip*. Almost every embroiderer enjoys making french knots, and closely packed together they give areas of crunchy texture. In stumpwork they can provide a way of raising the surface when worked as a separate slip, and applied in the same way as one worked on canvas. In a smaller ring frame, mount another piece of calico, and draw out a small motif which can be filled with french knots. Pack them together, covering the shape completely, and use a variety of threads in different thicknesses, contrasting matt and shiny ones. Small beads can also be interspersed between the knots to give added sparkle. It is advisable to make the outer edge as even as possible, since the whole area is to be cut out and applied to the sampler. (See Chapter 5.) Think of ways in which these slips could be used for a finished project. If two similar shapes were worked they could be joined

95 (*Opposite*) 'The White Tree'. Some slips of french knots have been applied, and the base has been padded with vilene (pellon) from the reverse side. The embroidery is worked in cream and white threads on a calico background. (*Vicky Lugg*)

96 A detail from a mirror frame, showing gooseberries which have been padded with felt and covered with satin stitch. The leaves are stitched flat to the surface. (*Barbara Dunhill*)

97 Another detail from the frame. The plums have been worked as canvas slips, and most of the leaves are stitched flat to the background. (*Barbara Dunhill*)

together, filled with animal wool, and attached to the background by a string of chain stitches or a buttonhole bar.

7 *Canvas slip*. Contrast the previous slip with one worked on a fine canvas using simple canvas work stitches, and remember that extra height can be given by padding the slip with animal wool. Insert the wool when the slip is two-thirds sewn in place, and then close the gap with small stab stitches. Try using a thick silk thread, which is well suited to work on a small scale.

8 Complete the sampler by working some of the raised stitches mentioned in Chapter 6. Try working groups of banksia roses in different thicknesses of stranded cotton, and see how many different variations can be made by using various weights of thread for raised cup stitch. Other stitches and ways of raising the surface will occur to you, so experiment, using your sampler as a notebook.

Now you are ready to begin on a finished embroidery with the necessary basic knowledge of which method and which stitches will give the effect you want.

8 Designing for modern stumpwork

Nowadays there is a much freer approach to embroidery, and many of the old rules are being broken. Experiments are made combining different techniques, and there is no reason why this should not be done provided the result is satisfactory, one technique serving to enhance another. A mixing of techniques can be very effective in raised work. It has, for instance, similarities with quilting, which is also raised from the surface, particularly in trapunto where only certain areas of the design are padded. Whitework and canvas work techniques are already an integral part of stumpwork, and perhaps these elements could be emphasized. An entire background worked on canvas might provide a good foil for raised motifs, where smooth surfaces could be contrasted with textured ones. For a small, delicate piece of work the emphasis could be placed on whitework methods, and if the embroidery were worked in whites and creams it would be even more effective. In fact, a technique known as Casalguidi (Castelguidi) combines either a drawn thread or pulled work background with raised flowers, stems and borders. The embroidery is usually in white on a strong-coloured ground, or natural on a natural-coloured fabric.

Metal thread embroidery combined with silk surface stitchery provides interesting contrasts, and there is no reason why some of the stumpwork methods cannot be incorporated as well. Padded shapes of layered felt, which are then covered, are common to both techniques. With all the mixed media experimentation that is part of embroidery now, the possibilities are endless.

The subject matter chosen by contemporary embroiderers covers a much wider field than that of the seventeenth century. Consequently it is very individual, and often reflects the style and personality of the worker. The examples shown in this book have been inspired by a variety of subjects; natural objects like flowers and foliage appeal to some, while others prefer to base their designs on figures, landscapes or more abstract themes. It is interesting to see the different applications of stumpwork, and although the embroiderers employ similar methods and stitches, each one has a personal approach, which is as it should be. How different from the seventeenth century, when only the quality of the needlework distinguished one embroidery from another.

Decorative boxes

The greater part of raised work today is mounted as panels, with mirror frames and caskets being in

98 'The Boundary Fence'. A fine leather is used for the background, and ribbons, wool pom-poms, bullion knots, french knots and detached buttonhole stitches have all been included to create an interesting texture. (*Jennie Parry*)

99 Cauliflowers on a market stall provided the starting point for this embroidery. The background has been sprayed with fabric dye, and french knot slips are applied and incorporated with quilting. The price tickets have been padded with vilene (pellon) and covered with calico. (*Mary Fortune*)

100 'The Old Man Of Parham'. The old and the new have been combined in this panel; the old man and the castle are directly inspired by seventeenth-century embroidery, but the treatment is contemporary. (*Mary Boughey*)

a minority. The elaborate cabinets with tiny drawers, secret compartments, and lift-out trays, although designed for practical purposes, seem to be a thing of the past. Instead, plastic art bins and boxes are thought to be more useful, though perhaps not so aesthetically pleasing. However, simply constructed boxes are still made and decorated with embroidery.

Ann Rutherford has made a modern casket purely as a decorative object (fig. 101), and describes how it was constructed.

'LITTLE PRECIOUS'

'Little Precious' has a papier mâché shell which was formed over an old wooden hat block. Before cutting the shell off the block, the positions of the waistlines and the necklines had to be considered so that there would be a natural break for the lid; this was done by sticking temporary paper figures around the shell. When this stage was complete the outside of the box was covered with cotton velveteen, and then the figures were stitched into place. A variety of fabrics were used and included leather, old tights, and two small sweaters which were knitted specially for the figures. All the hair and the fox fur were made with threads.

The lid was lined with quilted fabric on to which vague face shapes were drawn and embroidered. Since a baby's vision is limited, details were kept to a minimum. The crib, or pram, was anchored by invisible tapes so that it was not right at the bottom but suspended half-way down the box.

The intention was to portray an assortment of relatives, all (except for the one whose nose has been put out of joint) drooling over the new baby. The baby, surrounded by a halo of frillies, is red-faced and screaming, as babies are wont to be; probably terrified of the leering faces looming over it. Nevertheless, the aunties and grannies gaze even more adoringly through rose-coloured spectacles and murmur 'Little precious!'

This delightful casket proves that not everything has to be functional, and it seems an excellent way

101 'Little Precious'. A decorative box showing a family gazing adoringly at the new baby. The figures have been padded and dressed in a variety of contemporary clothes, even to the sweater carrying a slogan. See also colour pl. 10. (*Ann Rutherford*)

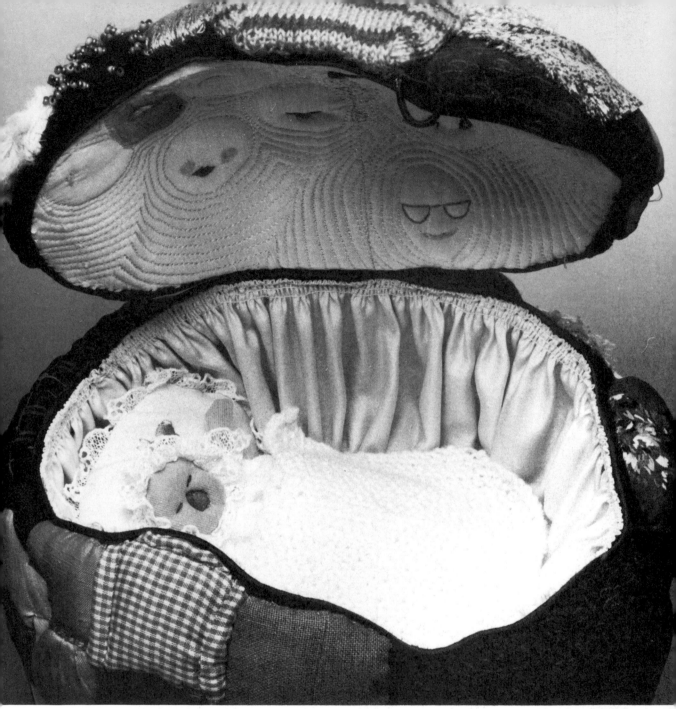

to commemorate a special event. Added attractions of 'Little Precious' are that one cannot help but smile at the small child sucking a thumb and clutching a blanket, surely a familiar sight to most mothers, and that when the lid is lifted it reveals the screaming infant, another all-too-vivid memory.

102 'Little Precious'. Another view of the box showing the baby, red-faced and crying in the cradle. (*Ann Rutherford*)
103 'Little Precious'. A close-up of the older child sucking a thumb and clutching a blanket for comfort. (*Ann Rutherford*)

104 'The Plain and Fancy Box'. A small box made from wood, left plain on the outside and with all the decoration on the inside. Satin stitch, french knots, detached buttonhole stitch and tiny pieces of mirror glass create a small garden. (*Margaret Rivers*)

105 A small round box with a design of grapes and vine leaves, worked in cream silks. The idea is based on a low relief carving which decorates the front of a house. The leaves are made from the same silk used to cover the box, the grapes are shapes cut from vilene and covered with satin stitch, and the flowers are clusters of french and bullion knots. (*Joan Matthews*)

Another much smaller box, which is also purely decorative, has been made by Margaret Rivers (fig. 104).

'THE PLAIN AND FANCY BOX'

The idea for this box came from seeing some concrete 'boxes' outside a modern building. Parts of them were covered with moss, lichen and tiny self-sown plants. The intention was to contrast this rich texture with the smooth surface of the

106 'An Edwardian Beach Scene'. The padded figures are covered with needlelace stitches and satin stitch. The hands are fashioned from covered wire. The embroidery is worked in sepia tones, giving the appearance of an old photograph. (*Barbara Hirst*)

thread. The trellis was sewn down on to a painted calico background and extra decoration was then added. A fine wire was wrapped with thread to make tendrils, and detached buttonhole stitch was again used to suggest other growth.

wooden box. The outside of the box was kept quite plain, and the decoration was revealed only when the lid was lifted.

The fabric used for the bottom and side panels was coloured with watercolour paints before being embroidered with a variety of silk, cotton and synthetic threads. Scraps of suede were applied to two of the side panels, and the base was slightly raised over card to simulate paving stones. Small pieces of mirror glass were stitched in place with detached buttonhole; this stitch has been used throughout to build up edges and other raised areas. French knots, seeding and straight stitches provide a contrast. Inside the lid is a 'trellis' made by wrapping wooden cocktail sticks with linen

Figures

Very different approaches to representing figures are shown in the illustrations, ranging from modestly dressed Edwardian ladies carrying parasols to the voluptuous figure of Eve coyly holding out an apple to Adam. In this particular panel (fig. 107), the embroiderer's sense of fun is very apparent. Patricia Sales's figures disport themselves in a leafy bower with the subversive serpent just in evidence coiling along the branch of the apple tree. The background material has been painted with fabric dyes, and leaves have been machine-embroidered on top. The tree trunk has been worked separately

107 'Adam and Eve'. The background has been painted with fabric dye and decorated with both machine and hand embroidery. The two figures have been cut from card, padded and covered with a fine stretch fabric. (*Patricia Sales*)

and applied to the background. Many of the leaves have also been machine-stitched, cut out and applied just by sewing them on at the tip so that they stand away from the surface. The serpent is slightly raised by covering vilene with a patterned fabric; the twinkling, glittering eyes are two small beads.

The figures of Adam and Eve are made from shapes cut from card, which have been padded with wadding and then covered with nylon tights. Their hair is made from embroidery thread. Tiny flowers have been made by cutting out shapes in fabric and attaching them to the background with a small bead.

'THE SPENCERS GARDENING'

Ann Sutton's small panel (fig. 108) shows two figures busy gardening. The man is digging with a spade and the woman is bending down to put

108 'The Spencers Gardening'. This small panel shows two figures busy in a garden. The figures have been slightly padded and detached buttonhole stitch has been used for the garments. A variety of stitches including fly, satin, seeding, and banksia rose has been used for the plants. See also colour pl. 7. (*Ann Sutton*)

109 'The Sea Captain'. A single figure padded and covered with stitching has been placed against a harbour wall, which has been made from padded shapes covered with satin stitch. (*Jenny Bullen*)

plants into a basket. The man is worked mostly in flat stitchery and only his hat, worked in detached buttonhole stitches, is raised from the surface. His hands clasping the spade are made from wrapped wire. The figure of 'Mrs Spencer' has been padded with felt and covered with detached buttonhole stitch; her basket is worked in a similar way but the stitching is in a thicker thread. Picots and banksia rose stitch have been used for some of the plants, and seeding and fly stitches have been worked in the background.

'THE COLLECTOR'

Wilke Smith gathers together a fascinating array of objects for her embroideries, and mixes techniques to achieve the result she requires. Her box, 'The Collector' (colour pl. 9), has been constructed of hand-made bark paper, with an arched aperture cut out to expose a background of black wool. The

110 'All My Own Work'. A design based on an open-air exhibition of paintings hung on railings. The 'paintings' have been made from canvas slips, and the artist has also been made separately and attached to the background. (*Mary Boughey*)

body of the figure is constructed from wool needlelace and the arms are made from wrapped threads. The tiny boxes are covered with either silk, paper or suede, and embellished with brass discs, shisha mirror glass and stitchery. At the top a stoneware tube spills out metallic threads and down feathers, and several pieces of native copper have been applied, all of which add to a very rich texture. The figure itself carries an assortment of objects of carved wood, copper and porcupine quills. The shiny and matt surfaces of the objects and the figure contrast with the neutral colour of the bark paper surrounding them.

111 Mirror frame. This is the complete frame from which previous areas have been isolated to illustrate points in the text. The design is based on fruits, most of which are raised from the surface using a variety of techniques and stitches. The embroidery is worked on fine linen in silk, stranded cotton, flower threads and *coton à broder*. The whole effect is one of variety and richness, and is an excellent example of the use of traditional methods in a contemporary way. See also colour pl. 6. (*Barbara Dunhill*)

Fruit and confectionery

One source of stumpwork design might be labelled 'eatables'. Fruit is especially popular, as some of the examples demonstrate. A magnificent garland of fruit surrounds a mirror frame made by Barbara Dunhill, which shows a very different approach to the traditional seventeenth-century frames. Some of the fruits have been worked as canvas slips and applied to the background, and padded to give extra height. Slips of french knots have been used for berries and there is an interesting contrast between smooth and textured areas, with flat surface stitchery for stems and leaves providing a foil to the raised motifs. Fine wool, stranded cotton and matt flower threads have been used for the embroidery. (See fig. 111.)

Apples form the basis of a small panel (fig. 112) treated in an entirely different way from the fruit in the mirror frame. Surface stitchery and metal threads are combined with trapunto quilting. A fine gold kid has been applied over layered felt, and some apples have been covered with detached buttonhole stitch. A background of straight stitches suggests a chequered cloth.

Blackberries, grapes and pineapples are all used by embroiderers in their designs, and seem particularly suited to raised work.

Colourful striped sweets are featured in the panel by Vicky Lugg which she has titled 'Sugared Almonds and Mixed Boilings' (fig. 116). A visit to a sweet shop stocked with boiled sweets in numerous colours and flavours provided the idea for this embroidery. Three jars sit on a shelf, each one containing a different kind of sweet. The jars and the shelf are made by cutting out the shapes in thick pelmet vilene and then covering them with fabric. The raised sweets are padded and covered with either satin stitch or french knots. Surface stitchery, using the same stitches, provides a contrast on some of the sweets. The background is sprayed with fabric dye and some stitching has been added to simulate wallpaper. The patterned and plain areas complement one another.

There is an air of Art Deco about the panel 'Ice-cream Parlour' (fig. 119). The design is based on ice-cream cones in assorted flavours. Again stitchery is combined with trapunto quilting, and some areas are raised by padding with thick vilene. Tiny seeding or speckling stitches provide a background, and the lettering is worked in back stitch using a shaded thread.

112 'Apples on a Check Cloth'. A chequered pattern of straight stitches provides the background for the apples. Trapunto quilting, felt and vilene (pellon) are all used to give a raised effect. Kid and metal threads are combined with silks to decorate the apples. See also colour pl. 12.

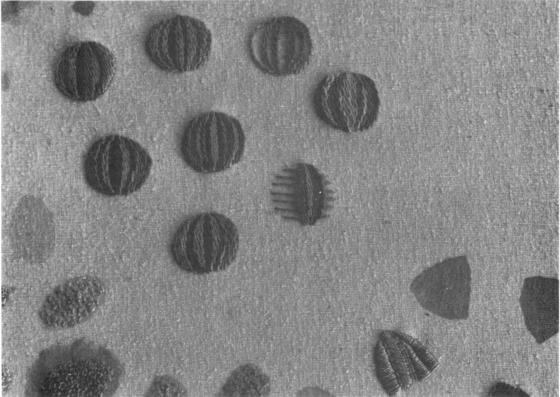

113 (*Top*) Sweets known as 'mixed boilings' provided inspiration for an embroidery using their bright colours and striped patterns.

114 Work in progress, showing some of the sweets worked separately as slips in raised stem stitch. When finished these were cut out and applied to the background. (*Vicky Lugg*)

115 'Sugared Almonds and Mixed Boilings'. The finished panel, showing three sweet jars sitting on a shelf. The background is sprayed with fabric paint using a stencil to make a trellis pattern, and some stitchery is added as further decoration. See also colour pl. 11. (*Vicky Lugg*)

116 Work in progress. The shape of the sweet jar is drawn out and the sweets worked either on the background or separately as slips to be applied. The jar filled with sweets is cut out, mounted over thick vilene (pellon) and applied to the background. (*Vicky Lugg*)

117 (*Opposite*) 'Pineapple'. Fruit again provides the source of design. The pattern of the pineapple segments is made by applying small pieces of gold kid and felt shapes which are covered in fine silk. The leaves are cut from suede. Silk and cotton threads are used for the stitchery.

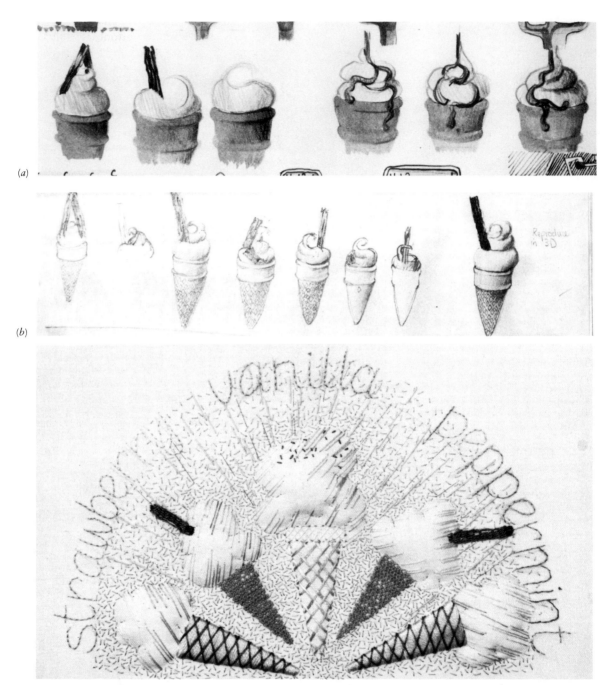

118 (a) & (b) (*Top and centre*) Studies of ice-cream cones in watercolour, and in pencil. (*Sarah Lugg*)

119 'The Ice-cream Parlour'. An assembly of cornets in a variety of flavours. Trapunto quilting and thick vilene (pellon) are used to raise the surface. Flat seeding stitch is used for the background, and stem stitch for the lettering. See also colour pl. 13.

Flowers and foliage

Flowers and foliage are a perennial source of design, whether treated in a formal, stylized way, or in a much freer and abstract manner. The small florets which make up the flower head, and the delicate nuances of colour, make the hydrangea a special favourite with embroiderers. In the panel worked by Christine Bloxham (fig. 120), the background of silk has been painted and part of the flower head is worked in french knots; some of these have been applied in the form of a slip. A few tiny beads are interspersed among the knots to give an added sparkle. Separate florets are worked either in satin stitch over vilene padding, or as free-standing motifs in detached buttonhole stitch worked over a framework of covered wire. Stranded cotton and silk thread has been used for the embroidery. The smooth satin stitch, worked in various directions, and the textured knots and buttonhole stitch, provide an interesting effect.

120 'Hydrangea'. Smooth satin stitch, french knots and detached buttonhole stitch give an interesting variety of textures to the embroidery. Some of the petals are worked on a framework of wire and stand away from the background; parts of the flower head are padded and worked as separate slips. See also colour pl. 8. (*Christine Bloxham*)

'POPPY PATTERN'

This panel, worked by Elizabeth Andrews, has a formal design of poppy seed heads in a vase contained within a stepped border (fig. 121). The vase has been worked in silk thread on a fine canvas and then applied to the linen background; padding has been added to raise it from the surface. The leaves have been worked over a framework of wrapped wire to make them free-standing, and above these are the stylized poppy seed heads. These have been padded with layers of felt and then covered with fine detached buttonhole stitch. Surrounding the vase of seed heads are two embroidered borders, the inner one worked in flat stitches, and the outer one in satin stitch, with berries slightly raised from the surface. The limited colour scheme of shades of green and brown gives a pleasing unity to the embroidery.

There are endless sources of inspiration for the embroiderer, from natural form to the man-made. No theme can be considered too ordinary, provided it is treated in an interesting and original way. Get into the habit of carrying a small sketchbook, one that will fit easily into a pocket or handbag, as ideas and inspiration can occur anywhere.

Having collected the information, you need to decide what it is that appeals to you about the subject and discard any details that are not really necessary to the design. It is best to aim for an

121 'Poppies'. A formal design in which the framing is an important feature, the main motif being recessed. The seedheads are padded and covered with fine detached buttonhole stitch and the leaves are worked over wire to stand away from the background. (*Elizabeth Andrews*)
122 (*Top right*) 'The Pergola'. A small finely stitched embroidery contrasting flat and raised stitchery. Small tendrils have been made by covering a very fine wire with thread, which has then been wound tightly round a needle. When the needle is withdrawn a small coil is formed. (*Barbara Buttle*)
123 Quarry rocks on the cliffs. The different layers and sizes of rocks provide a starting point for a small embroidery with padded and raised areas.

interpretation of the idea rather than a realistic representation.

Geometric form can be a good starting point and will help to overcome the problems of being too concerned with realism. Formal knot gardens are an excellent example, with the clipped box hedges laid out in formal patterns. Garden themes are always popular, from pergolas decorated with climbing plants to rockeries, pools and greenhouses. In gardening books, ideal garden layouts are often presented in diagram form looked at from above; this idea could be used as a starting point with the shrubs and flowers reduced to areas of pattern. Endless inspiration for shape, colour and texture can be found in landscape. The

124 Studies of snails found on the cliffs. Their rounded shapes and striped markings can suggest ideas for padded motifs.
125 Shells and pebbles have interesting shapes and patterns. These textured shells contrast well with the polished surface of the pebbles.

rounded forms of trees, stones and pebbles could be the basis for a design to include raised and padded areas. The strata of a cliff face with plants growing in the crevices between the rocks suggest a variety of surfaces and colours which can be interpreted in fabric and thread. Look at insects, snails, birds and animals, noticing their shapes and patterns. The delicate wings of insects, which are almost transparent, could suggest fine needlemade lace, while the rough woolly texture of a sheep could be seen as french knots. Observation and selection are of great importance in all design.

Examples of embroidery which reflect contemporary life can be found in the work being done by women in South America. The United States of America has set up a project in Peru to help supplement low incomes. The women make decorative textile pieces ranging from 30 cm (12 in.) to as much as 152 cm (5 ft) square, and the finished work is then sold abroad. The style is reminiscent of stumpwork, with heavily padded areas incorporated with hand stitched embroidery. Small padded figures are shown doing household chores, swimming, canoeing and dancing against a background of religious processions, orchards and vegetable gardens.

The pieces resemble the work which is being done by the women in Chile, who also sell their work abroad to help boost their meagre incomes. (See *Needle Arts*, the quarterly magazine of the Embroiderers' Guild of America, Fall 1985 issue.) They make small hangings called *arpilleras*, usually about 30 cm (12 in.) square, and worked in a combination of appliqué and simple embroidery stitches with an edging of crochet or blanket stitch. Small padded figures are often superimposed in a

126 (*Top right*) 'Quarry Cliffs'. A small panel based on drawings made of a Portland quarry, where plants grow out from the crevices between the rocks. Parts of the design are raised by using trapunto quilting which in places is covered with detached buttonhole stitch. Fly stitch, curl stitch and couching are used for the plants and smaller rocks.

127 A watercolour painting of a group of pebbles. The different sizes and shapes fitting together give ideas for design.

similar way to the seventeenth-century raised work. Aluminium foil is used for soldiers' helmets and little wooden toothpicks sometimes represent logs of wood. The Andes frequently feature as a backdrop to the activity of the figures in the foreground, who are shown doing all manner of tasks from household chores to going to market. These *arpilleras* reflect the poverty and hardship of the women's lives and have political overtones. An empty place at a table is an indication that one of the family is 'missing' from home. The recurring motif of the sun shining over the mountains can be interpreted as a symbol of hope.

Although these particular examples of raised work may lack coherent design and refinement of stitchery, they nevertheless provide a record of the people's lives just as much as the work of the seventeenth century.

128 (*Top*) 'A Rock Garden'. A variety of shapes and sizes of padded areas are used to give the effect of a rockery. Detached buttonhole stitch is used to cover some of the shapes, which are made either from padded felt or from old wooden button moulds. Wooden beads, smooth leather, and clustered french knots all help to add a rich texture. (*Jean Southwood*)

129 'Knot Garden'. A design of a garden with pebbles set among the plants. Again smooth surfaces contrast well with textured ones. Canvas work provides the background for the embroidery, and a variety of stitches and applied shapes are incorporated. (*Jacqui Bower*)

In conclusion, it must be said that there is always more to discover, and the fascination of embroidery is that one goes on learning all the time. However, it is all too easy to become serious and intense about something that is basically done for pure enjoyment. Stumpwork provides an ideal antidote, since it is fun to do, and if the result 'raises' a smile, so much the better. The embroiderers of the seventeenth century obviously enjoyed using their expertise to make pictures, caskets and mirror frames, and would no doubt have been delighted to know they had influenced their descendants so many years later.

130 (*Top*) 'Alpine Trough'. An embroidery based on a stone trough containing small alpine plants. The trough is constructed from card, padding and hessian, and a variety of fabrics including silk, wool, and leather are used for the plants. (*Jennie Parry*)
131 'Paved Garden'. Machine embroidery and hand stitching are combined in this panel. Some leaves are stitched flat to the background and others are worked separately, cut out and sewn on at just one point so that they hang freely. (*Ann Sutton*)

132 'The Cold Frame'. A completely three-dimensional embroidery which incorporates stumpwork techniques. The frame is constructed from card and covered with fabric. Acetate is used for the transparent top. (*Mary Fortune*)

133 A detail of some of the plants in the 'Cold Frame'. The flower pots, some only 1.2 cm ($\frac{1}{2}$ in.) in size, are carved from balsa wood. The plants are made either from fabric or from stitchery, using detached buttonhole on a wire framework. Since all the pots, seed trays and plants are free-standing they can be changed around at will, all of which adds to the charm of the piece. (*Mary Fortune*)

134 'The Dolphin'. A small finely stitched embroidery in delicate colours. The design is based on a decorative fountain with the cascade of water flowing from the mouth of the dolphin. Tiny french knots in fine threads and detached buttonhole chain are used for the splashing water, and the body of the dolphin is raised by trapunto quilting. Fly stitch is used for the tail and fins. (*Maureen King*)

135 'Sheep'. The whole panel is densely covered with stitching. Rows of woven picots form the leaves of the tree, the trunk of which is worked in raised stem band. The sheep are padded with felt and covered with detached buttonhole stitch, and their heads are carved from balsa wood and covered with silk. The inner frame is satin stitch over thick vilene (pellon). (*Barbara Dunhill*)

WHERE TO SEE EXAMPLES

There are many examples of seventeenth-century stumpwork in both museums and stately homes, and often in the latter they are tucked away in dark corners together with other artefacts of different periods. Occasionally one has the opportunity of seeing work from a private collection, and no doubt there are plenty more items packed away in attics waiting to be discovered.

The following list names just some of the more accessible places where examples of stumpwork are on display.

UK

Holborne of Menstrie Museum, Bath
Brecon Museum, Brecon, Powys
Cotehele House, Callington, Cornwall
Fitzwilliam Museum, Cambridge
Dorset County Museum, Dorchester
Burrell Collection, Glasgow
Fenton House, Hampstead
Temple Newsome House, Leeds
Victoria & Albert Museum, London
Whitworth Art Gallery, Manchester
Strangers Hall Museum, Norwich
Ashmolean Museum, Oxford
Lady Lever Art Gallery, Port Sunlight,
   Merseyside
Parham Park, Pulborough
Salisbury and South Wiltshire Museum,
   Salisbury
Warwick Museum, Warwick
Castle Museum, York

USA

Museum of Fine Art, Boston
Art Institute of Chicago
Concord Antiquarian Society, Concord, Mass.
Los Angeles County Museum of Art
Minneapolis Institute of Arts
Metropolitan Museum of Art, New York
Colonial Williamsburg, West Virginia

FURTHER READING

Beaney, Jan, *Stitches: New Approaches*, Batsford

Butler, Anne, *Encyclopaedia of Embroidery Stitches*, Batsford

Dawson, Barbara, *Metal Thread Embroidery* and *White Work Embroidery*, both Batsford

Howard, Constance, *Constance Howard's Book of Stitches*, Batsford

Lovesey, Nenia, *Technique of Needlepoint Lace*, Batsford

McNeill, Moyra, *Machine Embroidery: Lace and See-through Techniques*, Batsford

Practical Study Group of the Embroiderers' Guild, *Needlework School*, Windward

Springall, Diana, *Canvas Embroidery*, Batsford

Thomas, Mary, *A Dictionary of Embroidery Stitches*, Hodder and Stoughton

SUPPLIERS

Fabrics and threads can be bought at most large department stores. Wadding, tailoring canvas and vilene (pellon) are usually found in the department selling dressmaking fabrics. Small specialist embroidery suppliers will often provide a mail order service, and a current list of names and addresses can be found in *Embroidery*, the quarterly magazine of the Embroiderers' Guild.

Modelling clay, fine wire and balsa wood can be bought in specialist 'hobbies' shops and in most art shops, many of which have a section devoted to craft supplies. Vellum may also be found in art shops, with the calligraphy materials.

INDEX